INTERACTIVE
INSTRUCTIONAL
DESIGNS
FOR
INDIVIDUALIZED
LEARNING

INTERACTIVE INSTRUCTIONAL DESIGNS FOR INDIVIDUALIZED LEARNING

DANNY G. LANGDON

EDUCATIONAL TECHNOLOGY PUBLICATIONS
ENGLEWOOD CLIFFS, NEW JERSEY 07632

Printed in the United States of America.

Library of Congress Catalog Card Number: 72-89577.

International Standard Book Number: 0-87778-041-2.

First Printing

TO

BILL DETERLINE
my teacher

JACKIE HAMILTON
my student

PATRICIA, LISA, KIM
my source of inspiration

and many thanks to Zevart Shakarjian (and her husband, the proofer) for her quick and accurate typing of the final manuscript, and to Linda Shafer for typing from the original chicken scratch. Finally, a special note of thanks to the American College of Life Underwriters for providing the support and opportunity to explore the full range of what this mind can formulate.

PREFACE

The intent of this book is to provide a series of practical instructional designs that the reader may choose to replicate in meeting students' instructional requirements.

The need for this book is founded on the premise that implementors and designers of instruction generally know what is to be learned and through what channels (teacher, media); but they experience difficulty in deciding *how* to prescribe the instruction for actual use by students. It is the *how* that is the topic of concern in this volume.

The book opens with an explanation of what *is* an instructional design and what constitutes an *effective* instructional design. The chapters outline instructional designs to meet different instructional requirements. Each design is discussed in four parts: Use, Operational Description, Design Format, and Outcomes Expected. Interlaced in these topic headings is a discussion of how a particular design provides for individualized learning. The Appendices contain references on instructional technology and communications, and an outline of production procedures that should be followed in developing the different instructional designs.

Each instructional design was selected for its utility and ease of production. *Instructional designs requiring elaborate media hardware were avoided, as well as those which would generally require extensive time, expertise, or financial resources to produce.*

This book does not deal with how to write behavioral objectives, nor does it go into other detailed aspects of the techniques and principles of instructional technology. Many excellent books, monographs, articles, papers, and courses on the theory, rationale, and practice of how to produce effective instructional designs are available. It is more difficult, if not almost impossible, to find sources on what designs look like, what they do, and how they work. This *is* a text that contains practical instructional designs that have been produced, used, and validated. A certain degree of prerequisite knowledge on the reader's part is assumed, although this is minimal: some understanding of the principles behind stating student learning outcomes in behavioral terms. Each chapter was written to be a self-contained discussion about each design; and, therefore, a degree of redundancy will be noted in the discussion of certain concepts from one chapter to the next.

In summary, this is a handbook of instructional designs to be looked upon for their use, how they work, what they look like, and what outcomes can be anticipated, with special emphasis on individualizing learning.

Danny G. Langdon

CONTENTS

INTERACTIVE INSTRUCTIONAL DESIGNS FOR INDIVIDUALIZED LEARNING

CHAPTER I

THE EFFECTIVE INSTRUCTIONAL DESIGN

An instructional design is a format which prescribes student learning requirements and events. An effective instructional design is one that facilitates learning for students to the fullest extent possible. Such formats may include: prescriptions of instructional events for student use only; or a guide for teacher implementation only; or a prescription through which a medium presents instruction only; or a combination of these. If, for instance, it is said that a lesson plan is an instructional design, then a teacher-oriented implementation guide is suggested. Such a lesson plan can, however, specify certain interactive functions to be carried on with, or to be controlled by, the students.

It will be helpful in understanding what an instructional design *is*, if we first understand what it *is not*. For one, an instructional design is not media hardware—projectors, recorders, and other media devices. Media hardware are carriers (channels) through which instruction flows. Obviously, hardware has an influence on the effectiveness of instruction and should be chosen relative to such in presenting and reflecting intended student behavioral outcomes (learner objectives).

In the same sense that hardware is not an instructional design, an instructor or teacher also is not an instructional design. Like hardware, at least in part, a teacher is a carrier that implements instruction. The term carrier is in no way meant to be demeaning, as the most fortunate characteristic of this carrier lies in its flexibility and adaptive characteristics. The teacher has a set of "ears" to listen to students and a "mouth" to respond with in adapting to their learning problems. No one thus far has been able to equip a piece of hardware with "ears" that truly listen and a "mouth" that replies with an adaptive answer, other than in a "canned" fashion.

An instructional design is a format for learning. It constitutes a necessary step prior to the selection of the medium which will transmit the content of the design. The importance of making this distinction lies in the current emphasis that is placed on media acquisition and the claims by producers and sometimes users that such media are the *principal causes* of learning effectiveness. It is not unusual for schools and training departments to assume that the acquisition of a variety of media—and the more sophisticated the better—will bring about the solution to all instructional ills. In fact, it is often the case that *more emphasis should be given to effective instructional designs that actually format the instruction to and from students.*

The following communications model will illustrate the distinctive role which instructional design plays within the framework of instruction:

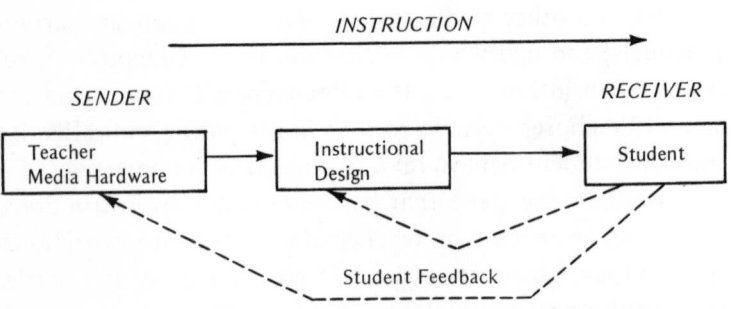

Requirements of an
Effective Instructional Design

A clearer definition of instructional design can be drawn by describing what constitutes an *effective* instructional design. This will be described on a generic basis, as it is the intent of this book to illustrate and discuss effective designs that can be replicated, rather than to discuss detailed procedures and techniques of design. Sufficient literature is available in other sources to learn and accomplish procedural requirements. A partial list of such sources is to be found in Appendix A.

The three basic requirements in achieving an effective instructional design are:

Behavioral Objectives
Interactive Instruction
Validation

Behavioral objectives, as the first requirement, relate to preplanning activities, and to a component to be used within the physical format of an instructional design. Interactive instruction is a technique and process written into an instructional design that is most often the reason for its effectiveness. Validation is a post-instructional design procedure for assuring that an instructional design *is* effective. To the extent that a design is not effective, validation includes the process of revising and retesting the instruction so that it becomes effective. As these three requirements are interrelated, it is difficult to conceive of them as being autonomous. However, for purposes of analysis each requirement will be discussed separately.

Behavioral Objectives

From a preplanning, predesign standpoint, behavioral

objectives are a *must*. When objectives are considered from the standpoint of whether they should be included in the implementation format of a design, that is, actually given to students, the debate among teachers and designers is unresolved. The author believes that objectives *should* be given to students, but we shall not argue the point here and now. However, when it comes to initiating the development of a design, that is, the planning phase for an intended instructional design, behavioral objectives are crucial. In simple terms, objectives are necessary so that you know *where* you are headed in designing; *how* you will get there and through *what* means; *how* you will provide for the students to get there; *how* the students will know when they have learned; and finally, *how* you can check to see that all such planning and actual design did achieve what it set out to do.

Within the sources listed in Appendix A are several excellent texts on how to analyze and express behavioral objectives. If you are unfamiliar with the concept of behavioral objectives, it is recommended that you check these sources closely. Assuming you are knowledgeable in the practice of specifying behavioral objectives, let us proceed to the question of why behavioral objectives are so important in the process of producing effective instructional designs.

Behavioral objectives give the designer the indicators of what behavior, conditions, and standards must be planned and provided within the design. The design requirements for a behavior involving manual manipulation of items are obviously different from those for a behavior involving mental discrimination (identifying similarities and differences).

In discussing this need for specifying behavioral objectives in the planning stage of instructional design, it would be a mistake not to include other considerations that relate to objectives. Such considerations as student entry level characteristics, physical facilities, and administrative constraints and requirements also have their effect on the planning and ultimate effectiveness of an instructional design. Although these will not be discussed in this text in any detail, they should be kept in mind, as they relate to the topic of objectives in general.

Now, what about the role of objectives when an instructional design is actually being used by students and/or implemented by a teacher?

First and foremost, objectives communicate clearly to the student what he is to learn. In effect, they tell him where he should direct his attention both in terms of content to be learned and the behavioral change that must occur. If it is a teacher who is implementing the instruction, then the teacher would know what content is to be presented and what behavioral change must occur.

Clearly defined objectives also serve some other valuable functions during implementation. Objectives may specify or imply the stimuli which the student should attend to as the signal for the behavior to take place.

Finally, objectives may set standards which a response must meet to be acceptable. This, too, is a part of instructional design implementation. Related to this setting of standards is the need to provide in the instructional design the confirming feedback which tells the student he has or has not mastered the objective. Feedback, in turn, is related to the concept of reinforcement and reward.

One aspect of the role of objectives in implementation deserves special mention. This relates directly to the value of objectives in individualizing learning. Objectives communicate to the student what he is to learn. In effect, they are targets to be aimed at and achieved. If properly stated in clear terms, they also tell the student when he has accomplished mastery of the objective. In any attempt at individualizing learning, communication to the student that he has learned is critical.

For many of the designs given in this book, student self-recognition of when he has learned is a necessity. For instance, the design called Learner Controlled Instruction suggests giving the student a list of objectives, with specific content references. The student pursues the study of references towards an objective until he "thinks" he has gained satisfactory performance of that objective—and then he requests testing to find out for certain. An unclear objective or only a content description would make this particular instructional design unworkable for student use, and would negate the individualized learning aspect of the design.

Interactive Instruction

The major problem with a lecture as an instructional design is that it is not interactive instruction. A lecture is one-way instruction, from lecturer to student. The lecture provides a simple illustration to explain that interactive instruction is a two-way matter—from teacher or media to student *and* from student to teacher or media.

You might immediately question how a student could possibly interact with *media*. However, don't confuse your reasoning by thinking that the student is going to talk to the medium. What interaction means is simply that the implementor asks questions, even if it is via an audio or visual projection, and the student responds. This is the start of interaction. In the case of a teacher, the student obviously can ask his own questions or give a response. This is more interaction. In the case of media, the medium itself can ask questions, and can provide confirmation and possibly multiple branches to other information and questions to which the student can respond. This, too, is a kind of interaction, although obviously more limited than when a teacher is present. These various means all help to provide interaction.

By the term "interaction" we are not limited just to responses as specified by the behavioral terms of an objective. Included also are those activities related to practice. Not all objectives are a one-shot, one-response affair. Practice sharpens behaviors, and thus interactive practice, so to speak, must often be included in the instructional design.

There are a number of other considerations related to providing for interactive instruction, some of which will become obvious as each design is presented. The references found in Appendix A suggest others.

Validation

Validation has been aptly described as a "debugging" process. It can be viewed as either a post-design or in-process method of designing activity, depending on time and need for implementation. Hopefully, it would be the latter. More specifically, validation is testing to see that the students who have experienced an instructional design have in fact *learned.* Where learning has not been effective, under validation procedures, *the instruction is revised and tested again until learning is effective.*

Validation testing is based on the objectives, for such testing is designed to test *every* objective. Where objectives are not achieved, the instructional designer then goes back into the instruction and finds out why. Failure to go back into the design and determine *why* will only result in the continued implementation of some ineffective segments of instruction. Validation procedures are discussed in several of the references listed in Appendix A.

Chapter Summary

Effective instructional designs are developed around principles and techniques related to behavioral objectives and interactive instruction. The assurance that a level of learning effectiveness has been achieved from a design is verified by validation procedures. Objectives tell the designer where he is going in terms of expected student outcomes. Interactive instruction relates learning events to the objectives and seeks to involve students in the instructional design to the fullest extent possible. The process of validation checks for effectiveness and provides for removing and revising ineffectiveness. The instructional designs which follow are built around these three principles and techniques.

CHAPTER II

LEARNER CONTROLLED INSTRUCTION

Use

One of the most versatile and flexible instructional designs is Learner Controlled Instruction (LCI). Within this design many other instructional designs can function, including those based upon existing instructional materials. Thus, LCI may be said to be a "grand design" which incorporates many other existing and specially written designs. It is this capability to use existing materials that provides its flexibility factor.

LCI is used in an individualized learning environment. However, it may be applied within more group-oriented programs. For instance, LCI can be used in a laboratory setting, such as in science and language labs. A segment of group instruction can be converted to LCI and covered in a relatively short time span.

Operational Description

The words that make up the name of this design denote its meaning and how it functions—it is *instruction controlled by the student*. The student is placed in a learning environment in which he is given *freedom* to do the following:

1. From a list of behavioral objectives which outline the behavioral outcomes expected of the student, the student himself is allowed to select that objective or set of objectives

he wants to learn first. He is given the opportunity to select objectives in terms of his own interests, for whatever motives and for whatever reasons. Selecting an objective or set of objectives is the first exercise of the learner's control.

2. Having selected an objective, the student then uses whatever resources of information or instruction are available. This is a selection process that he again controls in terms of what he feels would be of most value towards learning a particular objective. As will be shortly elaborated upon, this includes a great variety of resources—ranging from a resource person (expert, teacher, etc.), through media of all kinds, to text material. The key requirement is that the student is afforded the right to select or reject whatever resources are specified or can be found on his own.

3. When the student has taken as much time as he deems necessary to learn the objective, he can request to be tested on his ability to perform the objective as specified. Again, the learner controls instruction, this time in terms of *when* he will be tested. In effect, he is saying, "Test me now, I am ready; don't wait another day, week, or until the end of the semester; I'm ready NOW!"

In a more descriptive manner, Learner Controlled Instruction operates as follows: The learner is given a list of objectives for the course. These objectives describe all the behavioral outcomes he must master to complete the course. It might well be that in certain courses this means all the objectives and in others a minimum number of objectives, with any beyond this number as additional "credits."

The critical requirements in the specification of objectives are: first, that they be measurable, so that some evaluator, such as the teacher, may ultimately observe whether the student can demonstrate that he has learned; and second, that they communicate to the student a behavioral change "intent," so that the student is given direction in his learning effort; he knows what to learn and how to demonstrate after learning that he has indeed learned. Obviously, the objectives cannot be too large or too small in their specification of behavioral intent.

Thus far in the operation of an LCI design we know that the student has a list of objectives. As the second step, he then reads the required objectives and decides which he would like to learn first. (There may also be "nice-to-know," enrichment objectives, which can be approached following mastery of basic, required work.) He decides upon an order, according to his immediate and long-range interests and needs related to other objectives he will be learning. It would be unrealistic to think that this selection process is not governed at times by certain limitations. For instance, suppose the student has selected and been tested on all the objectives which he found most interesting. He must now work on those objectives that do not particularly appeal to him, but still must be mastered as basic course requirements. As another possible limitation on the selection process, the student may well select an objective for which another objective is a prerequisite. On this particular point, the student generally finds out for himself quickly that prerequisites exist. To suppose that the designer of instruction always knows the best sequence and will therefore prescribe that sequence may not prove to be valid. This is particularly true for an instructional setting in which a large number of students are involved, and an attempt is made to prescribe a sequence for all. At a minimum, in the validation of an LCI program with many students, certain prerequisites should be allowed to emerge based on actual student use. Experience in the use of this design has shown that students develop many paths to an objective which has prerequisites. In simple terms, "there's more than one way to skin an instructional cat." Allowing students to exercise their own interest in the selection of which objectives to study first will enhance the students' self-motivation and attention to learning.

There are other factors which might also influence student selection of objectives. These include the availability of certain materials, utilization of resource persons, and scheduling problems.

Having selected his objective(s), the student then proceeds to activities related to learning. To do this he needs resources, materials, and other learning "tools" which contain the content related to the objective. To give the student some assistance, known resources, including the teacher, aides, community people, and instructional materials are keyed to each objective. The student on his own may well find other resources and materials through such sources as the library.

It is important to note that in utilizing resources and materials, the student exercises complete control over what he will use. This also means he can reject whatever he feels is irrelevant. As mentioned above, resources could include the teacher, films, books, experiments, on-the-job training, or whatever. He might even use community resources. The intent is to reach a point where the student feels he has learned the behavior outlined in the objective on which he is working. Once he feels he's got it, it only remains to be seen if in fact he does. This leads to the third component of the LCI design—testing. But, before leaving the resources and materials, it should be noted that the student may well have selected an objective he can already perform. He has the existing knowledge or skill, and can skip the step of consulting lists of resources. In this case, he can request immediate testing. This is but one of the reasons why LCI is efficient.

When a student determines that he has gained the capability to perform an objective as specified, he requests to be tested. To fulfill this request, a test is needed—and a means of confirming his test results. The test is not always just a test in the normal sense of what we think of when we say "test." Whatever the objective specifies in the way of a behavioral change is the guide to the "test." If it is the skill of manual manipulation, he should be tested by manipulation. If it is a discrimination behavior, then he should select or possibly check off items from a written list. If it is an oral behavior, he should speak it. However, if a simpler form of testing has been shown to be a reliable and valid indicator of the behavior outlined in the objective, the simpler form of testing may be used, i.e., a written test indicates the same as an oral test on a given behavior. This is determined through . validation procedures. As for the means of confirmation of the test results, an evaluator is normally used; this could be the teacher, as in most instances, or a third party.

Finally, when a student has demonstrated satisfactory performance in a test situation, he moves on to another objective or continues with other objectives he has been working on concurrently. If he fails to perform on a given objective, he goes back and seeks other sources or goes over already-used sources until he feels he is again ready to be tested.

The essential operating characteristic of Learner Controlled Instruction is, of course, learner control. To summarize, this control by the learner begins with selecting objectives and continues with resource selection and use. Finally, control is exercised in deciding when he feels he is ready to be tested. Many desirable outcomes can be expected from using LCI, but first let us look at the physical format design within which LCI operates.

Design Format

The instructional design format for LCI is composed of four basic parts:

Objectives with Keyed Resources
Criterion Tests
Student Guide to LCI
Evaluator Guide to LCI

(In the final format, the Objectives with Keyed Resources may be combined with the Student Guide as one package.)

Objectives with Keyed Resources

This component of the LCI design contains the list of all objectives, stated in measurable terms. To each objective, all existing reference materials are keyed. References can be of any kind, from people to films, texts, recordings, and so forth. Figure 2.1 illustrates a format for the objectives, with keyed resources.

Figure 2.1

III. STARTING PLANTS

H.   *Rooting Media and Equipment*
      Goal: Upon completion of this unit, you will be able to properly prepare rooting media, understand the need for proper media to assure plant growth, and be familiar with the tools and container requirements for growing plants prior to planting in open ground.

Objectives	Proposed Completion Date	Criterion Test	Completion Date	Verification
1. List a minimum of five moisture-holding substances that can be used as rooting media for cuttings (MF-Chap. 9, SWGB-p. 81, SGC-pp. 16-17).		TW		
2. Describe two methods for sterilizing soil when soil is intended for use in a rooting mixture (MF-Chap. 9, F-"Better Gardens").		TO		
3. In terms of either ratios or percentage, list the component breakdown of at least two commonly used mixtures used as rooting media (MF-Chap. 9, Pamphlet-"Potting Plants").		TW		
4.				

In this format, objectives are listed under appropriate major topics. Each topic is given some refinement by a statement of a generic goal which indicates the general behavioral requirements to be mastered by the student. Following the generic goal are the detailed behavioral objectives. These are the specific behavioral objectives to be achieved by the students. Although numbered in this format, these objectives are not sequenced, unless there is a specific requirement that calls for a sequence such as indicated by the results of validation testing. It was stated above that students may select objectives in any order. To specify a sequence when in reality there is no necessity or requirement for such a sequence is to destroy the first key aspect of Learner Controlled Instruction—that is, student control.

Immediately after each objective, resources are keyed. Keying may appear, if desirable, in a separate column to the right of each objective. References can be keyed as to the type as well as the location of the reference, i.e., "F" might denote a film.

The four columns to the right of the objectives are for recordkeeping and informational purposes. The first column, entitled Proposed Completion Date, serves the purposes of planning. When a student selects an objective or set of objectives, he should give the teacher or course monitor some indication of when he "thinks" he will complete the objective. This is not to say that this date is an absolute requirement for completion of the objective. It serves the purposes of having the student make plans for what he is going to have as a target date, and of giving the teacher an idea of when resources of a special nature will be needed—as well as when to anticipate a student request for criterion testing. However, in an instructional setting in which time is a highly restrictive factor, the proposed completion date may well become a necessary completion date. If this type of rigidity can be avoided, do so by all means. As a cue to one of the outcomes to be expected in the use of this particular instructional design, time is typically reduced. This might be contrary to what one might have thought, but it will be seen below how this is achieved.

The "Criterion Test" column is informational in nature. It tells the student what kind of test will be used to measure his performance on an objective. The kinds of tests illustrated in this format are indicated by the initials:

TW—Written Test

TO—Oral Test

P—Performance Test, such as a manipulative skill

FP—Final Product Test (used for objectives in which a report or complex product is to be produced, requiring much time or which can be done on a one-time-only basis, analogous to a term project, report, etc.)

The "Completion Date" and "Verification" columns are self-explanatory. A record should be kept of when the student actually completed an objective. This gives the student and teacher some idea of how long it takes to learn certain kinds of objectives. This is valuable information for future planning by student and teacher alike. The "Verification" column is for the evaluator's (teacher, monitor) sign-off of the student who has successfully completed the objective.

A final note to the *Objectives with Keyed References* section: It is usually necessary to have two copies of the document shown in Figure 2.1—one for the student's use and one for the program monitor's file.

Criterion Tests

As previously stated, the criterion tests are usually of

four types—written test (TW), oral test (TO), performance test (P), and final product (FP). Other classifications are possible. The author has found these of particular use in his own instructional design requirements and needs. A sample of a criterion test is shown in Figure 2.2. Each of the other three types is essentially set up in the same manner as this TW test.

In the upper left corner appears the code to the kind of test required. A "TW" would be given if the student is to write his answers. A "TO" would be retained by the evaluator and read to the student. A "P" test would be either given to the student or read to him. A "FP" test would normally be a checklist retained by the evaluator and used at the time the student presents his final product for inspection and evaluation. TO and P tests are usually in the form of checklists as well.

Figure 2.2

TW   III-H-5

Criterion Test

Name   ....   Date ....

Certain types of chemicals can be used to treat wooden flats in order to prevent wood decay. Which of the following are correct chemicals to use?

........A.   Copper Naphthenate
........B.   Cuprinol
........C.   Isopropyl Alcohol
........D.   Petroleum
........E.   Varnish

In the upper right corner is a code to the objective of which this particular criterion test is a measure. In the illustration, III is the major topic heading, H is the subtopic, and 5 is the number of the objective. Reference to Figure 2.1 will show how this test has been coded to the objectives. The purpose of this coding is simply one of administrative convenience, so that a test can be easily located when needed.

The remaining parts of the criterion test format are self-explanatory, containing a blank for the student's name, the date, and finally the test itself.

In the case of TO, P, and FP criterion tests, checklists are normally used so that the evaluator can "check" each item as the student demonstrates (TO and P) or exhibits for inspection (FP) his mastery of the objective. As an additional consideration, it might be desirable to specify somewhere on this test the number of items that must be checked off as a standard of satisfactory performance. The standard could, of course, be all items on the checklist.

In the case of TO and P criterion tests, special instructions must be specified for the evaluator as guides to how he should administer the tests. These are usually specified in the criterion test as oral instructions to be given by the evaluator to the student. For example, for Objective 2 (Figure 2.1), instructions on the criterion test would be to inform the evaluator to tell the student to "Describe the two methods for sterilizing soil when soil is intended for use in rooting mixtures." Thus, for TO, P, and FP criterion tests, instructions and a checklist of what to observe are the usual design requirements.

The criterion tests are contained in a separate folder or file. They are administered for distribution by the evaluator. In certain instances, depending on the nature of the instructional setting, criterion tests might be kept out in the open. Multiple copies of the TW tests will be needed to serve many students, as each student actually writes on the test itself—unless the TW tests are multiple-choice, true-false, or matching, in which case a single copy can be used, with answer sheets. Only one copy of TO, P, and FP tests is usually needed. Completion of these tests, as with the TW, is recorded on the Objectives with Keyed Resources Form.

Student Guide to LCI

It will be necessary to provide students with a guide describing what LCI is and how it works. The outline of the more detailed contents of such a guide might be as follows:

I   What is Learner Controlled Instruction?
II   How LCI works
    A.   General Description
    B.   Components
       1.   Objectives
       2.   Criterion Tests
III   Responsibilities of the Evaluator
    A.   Program Administration
    B.   As a Resource Person
    C.   As an Evaluator of Criterion Tests
IV   Responsibilities of the Student
    A.   Objectives and Planning
    B.   References and Resources
    C.   Criterion Tests
       1.   TW (with example)
       2.   TO
       3.   P
       4.   FP
V   General Procedural Guide (checklist)

The body of this outline can be filled in with many of

the descriptions as already provided in the foregoing discussion of LCI. After validation testing, the Student Guide can be combined with the Objectives with Keyed Resources as one component.

Evaluator's Guide to LCI

The evaluator's guide contains the same basic information as the student's guide. One item of particular importance that should be elaborated upon is how the evaluator or program monitor acts as both a resource person and an evaluator:

As a resource person, he acts at the will of the student. The student views the resource person as another source of information and instruction, much the same as a text or film. As such, the student can request and reject information according to his own needs, not the resource person's estimate of what is best and what is not. If the resource person had an on-off switch, the student in this instructional design could make good use of it, which is not to say that students using other kinds of instructional designs do not also wish that they had such a magical switch. The point is, the use of a resource person, be it the teacher or someone else, lies solely in the hands of the student. The student is the controller of instruction.

The evaluator should be cautioned to evaluate in terms of the objectives. This is crucial, since the objectives are the student's guides as to how and what to perform. The student is directing his learning effort in the direction of the behavior specified in the objectives, and therefore he must be tested on *that* behavior and not some other behavior. There must be no surprises.

Outcomes Expected

It was stated in the opening paragraph of this chapter

that LCI is one of the most versatile and flexible instructional designs. This statement is true not only in regard to the operation of LCI, but also in the outcomes to be expected from its use. Many of the outcomes are stated below, but do not be surprised to find many others during implementation.

First, students who have been exposed to this type of instructional design typically emerge with a much higher level of self-confidence. Why is this so? In the first place, the students are continually involved in decision-making. They must select objectives, control their resources, and achieve to their own satisfaction a level of performance that is adequate to pass the criterion tests. Within this, they must get to know the resources available to them. The library, for instance, truly becomes a resource center of much useful information. The resource person must be confronted directly for information, rather than indirectly as a lecturer. A closer relationship between student and resource person is possible. For these reasons and others, the student gains confidence.

The second outcome to be expected is that instructional time typically is reduced. This is probably contrary to what one would normally think to be the case. Implementation of LCI has, nevertheless, shown that instructional time is reduced. The main reason for this is that the students do not have to concern themselves with *irrelevant sources or content.* In addition, they can make use of existing skills. For instance, they may already know a particular objective and can request immediate testing. The testing itself is reduced in that they can be tested when they wish rather than on a mass basis—and often without supervision.

As a third outcome, the time required of teachers and other subject matter resource people is typically reduced, as such resources are used on an "as needed" basis. What is increased is the resource person's need to sharpen his capabilities to meet each student's demands. The resource person finds himself having to "really know" his subject, because students are working on various objectives, and they demand different information at different times. In instructional situations where existing on-the-job personnel are used as resource persons, there is the added advantage of such persons having to keep up on the latest developments in their own fields.

Fourth, it is not necessary for all students to begin a course at the same time, because each student chooses his own route to accomplish the objectives.

Fifth, if implemented in the optimum, most individualized setting, the student should develop a more positive attitude towards learning. This is simply because the students are not competing against one another. Rather, they are learning towards external criteria. Students may ultimately be "graded," but it is the process of learning itself with which they are concerned; and, working on different objectives, they do not have to compete with one another.

Finally, in terms of the teacher-evaluator, his job becomes more clearly defined. The more typical functions of a teacher are retained in LCI in that he is still a resource person and evaluator. More importantly, however, he becomes a "teacher" in that he must become involved with each student on a one-to-one basis, according to the needs and desires of the student.

CHAPTER III

INTERACTIVE LESSON PLAN

Use

In part, because the title of this instructional design is "lesson plan," it implies a teacher's prescription of student learning events. However, the use of the term "interactive" in conjunction with "lesson plan" adds a dimension related directly to *the students who will experience the instructional events* rather than the teacher who uses the lesson plan.

The effectiveness of group-oriented instruction often suffers from a lack of continuity from one class setting to the next. Even the most experienced teacher has been aware that his or her presentation varies in *quality* from class to class. The problem of quality, as with other problems associated with group instruction, is even more apparent when viewed from the standpoint of the students.

For one thing, students generally experience difficulty ascertaining the "critical content" of a lesson plan presentation. Even the task of taking notes goes far beyond desirable limits, so that some content is totally missed and other content is recorded incorrectly. Furthermore, related to this attempt to acquire and record the content is a general lack of continuous responding that allows a student to assess his own progress. Also missing is feedback which tells the student he has responded correctly or incorrectly. The general lack of both relevant responses and feedback is not only a student problem in terms of assessing his own learning progress, but also a teacher problem—the teacher has difficulty assessing individual and general group progress during instruction and adapting to it quickly when progress is not being achieved.

In general, a lesson plan does attempt to deal with the problem of continuity in instruction. There is usually an outline of content, examples, and practice exercises in a sequence for the teacher to remember for presentation. The student problems associated with *identifying critical content, active responding,* and *feedback* are the components most often overlooked in the usual lesson plan. An interactive lesson plan, on the other hand, such as the one suggested in this chapter, overcomes these problems.

Even an interactive lesson plan is teacher oriented. It is important, therefore, that the prescription of instruction within the lesson plan be stringent in prescribing what must occur, yet flexible, so that interaction can take place.

A "canned" interactive instructional design (i.e., film, recording) will be presented the same way every time. Content, required interactions, and confirmations will not be left out. Compare this to a teacher presentation via a lesson plan wherein each lesson is not presented the same way every time. In the teacher lesson plan there exists a double-edged sword of flexibility—the highly desirable capability of the teacher to adapt to student learning needs, with a flexibility that might mistakenly not provide students with all the interaction and content they need to achieve course objectives.

Finally, an interactive lesson plan is not simply a script to be read by a teacher. It is a sequence of topics to be discussed—but always aimed at the behavioral objectives to be achieved by the students. At appropriate points, the teacher asks questions to provide students with the opportunity to assess their own learning and to provide valuable feedback to the teacher on individual and class progress. Such questions are usually in a workbook for student use. Feedback in the way of confirmation for correctness of responses is provided so that adaptation to student needs can follow.

Operational Description

The instructional setting is the classroom. There are two parties, each of which has requirements of its own. Yet, the requirements must work in unison to achieve the maximum in effective learning. The first set of requirements relates to the student; the second is for the teacher.

For the Student:

1. The opportunity must exist for students to know *what* is going to happen. The best way to communicate this is by the use of behavioral objectives. These statements key the student to what is relevant, and thus what to attend to. More importantly, they describe how and on what he must perform following the instruction.

2. Second, the student should be allowed to prepare for what is going to happen in the classroom. He should work in advance so that he can understand more readily and be prepared with his own questions. Although this preparation for instruction is not actually a part of the lesson plan itself, it is worth mentioning here, and can be resolved by other instructional designs discussed elsewhere in this book.

3. The student needs something to interact *with*. While much of the interaction could be fulfilled by the interaction (questions) initiated by the teacher, a copy of the interaction in the way of a *workbook* is more appropriate. *Within the workbook the student will complete questions and write notes of his own interpretation of the content presented.* The workbook becomes a recordkeeping device of much value for review later on. More importantly, it is a means for

responding that demonstrates the student's having acquired the learning that is presupposed to be taking place.

4. The student needs feedback. This provides a direct assessment of the correctness of responses. It is particularly important to provide feedback to students so that, when they find they have made an incorrect response, they will be prompted to seek additional instruction that will then bring them to the point of being correct. Feedback can be provided within the workbook as well as directly by the teacher.

For the Teacher:

1. The same set of student behavioral objectives given to students must, of course, be used by the teacher. While this sounds simple, it is often not followed in practice. For implementation, the objectives are sequenced; but the instructional design format to be suggested will allow for some flexibility of sequence.

2. Content reminders are needed relative to each objective. One of the reasons why a teacher has a lesson plan in the first place is that he or she needs some quick reference to content that must be presented. Content should be closely tied to the objectives to be served. Content is not only word descriptions, but the variety of media forms that can also *present* content.

3. Clarification content is included, such as illustrations and examples to make the content clear. Much of this often takes the form of visual illustrations.

4. Directions are essential as to when and what responses will be elicited from students. This is the "structured" interaction between what the teacher has said or done to the content and what the student *interprets* as having been said or done. It is the opportunity for the student to show that he has learned. For the teacher, it is the opportunity to assess the effectiveness of instruction. Such performance is generally accomplished by answering questions within the work-

book, but may also include performance by manual manipulation and oral presentation.

5. Students are directed to respond; and, having responded, are told if their responses are correct. When correct, the students know they have learned correctly, and the teacher knows he can move on to the next sequence of instructional events. When incorrect, the flexibility of the teacher can allow for further clarification and additional responding.

For Student and Teacher Together:

The basic problem with the usual lesson plan is that it is not "response" oriented. It does not have the means for a continual assessment of whether the students are learning what the teacher *tells them*. It does not allow the student to respond. The usual lesson plan is stimulus oriented—information from the teacher. It should be *both* stimulus and response oriented.

To say that the usual lesson plan is stimulus oriented is not to say that a teacher does not have the students in mind when the lesson plan is drawn up. Certainly the teacher is trying to plan a sequence of instruction that is effective, with relevant illustrations and descriptions that students can readily understand. What is generally lacking is the opportunity for students to *show* that they understand. It is common to say to the students, "If you don't understand what is being presented, then ask questions." Rather than placing the burden directly on the students, interactive instruction deliberately places the burden on the implementor to find out, and the student only (only!) to show that he can perform. Having students respond to existing questions in a workbook, called structured interaction, is itself more apt to cause the student to ask his own questions than would otherwise be the case—when told to ask questions if he "feels" he is having difficulty. He will want to know why he was wrong.

The student and teacher requirements have been discussed separately, but how do they work together? The starting point is the set of behavioral objectives. They represent what the student must learn and what the teacher is to instruct towards. That is, student *learning* and teacher *implementation* are directed at the objectives. Students read a set of objectives for a particular unit of instruction. The teacher then initiates a presentation of content relative to one or more objectives. Illustration by means of visuals or use of the familiar blackboard can serve to clarify content presented. As this is being done, the students may ask questions of their own. Finally a point is reached, according to an assessment by the teacher, when the content directed at an objective has been covered and the students have learned. The teacher then must find out if they have learned. This is accomplished by directing the students to answer a question or series of questions in their workbooks; or it might take the form of actual performance, as in the case of manipulative or oral presentations. The students then answer or perform. The teacher can now either ask the students to give their responses or could, in certain instances, simply confirm their response with the correct answers. The confirmation for some questions might even appear *in the workbook*, rather than coming from the teacher. Flash (colored) cards, raising the hand, oral response, or a variety of other means might be used to indicate student responses. All of this is feedback to the teacher, indicating whether learning has taken place; and for the students, confirmation of their having learned. For areas of student difficulty, the teacher has the flexibility to branch to additional clarifying content or additional practice. When satisfactory performance is finally achieved by the students, the teacher then moves on to other objectives, content, clarification, and student responding. This is interactive instruction within a lesson-plan approach.

Design Format

The design format of an interactive lesson plan can vary. However, two basic requirements must be covered: (1) a means for students to record their responses and (2) a means for guiding the interaction and presenting instructional information. *There should be a student workbook and a teacher lesson plan.* The design recommended in this chapter accomplishes both requirements. It can be used both by those who are designing lesson plans for their own use and those planning lesson plans to be implemented by others.

To summarize, there are two components to the interactive lesson plan: (1) the student response means (a workbook), and (2) the lesson plan itself.

There are five basic parts to both the student workbook and the teacher lesson plan. These parts must be viewed as a whole.

Student Workbook

Since it is the student to whom the instruction is being directed, the *student workbook* will be discussed first. The five parts of the workbook are:

Purpose and Significance
Objectives
Questions
References
Notes

Purpose and Significance

Figure 3.1 illustrates a Purpose and Significance section of an interactive lesson plan. Students should know why they are about to be exposed to some particular learning requirements. The general intent in this section is to project to the student some *affective* qualities to their learning. It states the *why* of the unit of instruction. And this *why* is stated in generic, goal-directed terms, such as: will understand, appreciate, become familiar with, and so forth.

Within job-oriented instructional programs, the Purpose and Significance section is vitally important for relating the instruction to the job to be performed. Within academic courses, the same essential point of relating the instruction to some values, an overall sense of how it helps to better the individual, or similar goal, is important. The statements contained in the Purpose and Significance section are an attempt to answer the question often asked by the student: "Why should I study this stuff?" The intended outcome is both content orientation and student motivation.

Figure 3.1

Some Techniques for Improving In-Class Effectiveness

Purpose and Significance

The purpose of this segment of instruction is to introduce you to some techniques for improving in-class effectiveness. This title is somewhat misleading in that the techniques to be introduced relate to pre- and post-class activities as well. The use of the word "some" is appropriate because, in the short period of time available, only a few major techniques can be "introduced."

What you will gain are some techniques that can be utilized immediately; with some practice, others can be used in time. Most of the suggested techniques are readily useable. Others require some time to prepare. If you can find time to use only a couple of the techniques, we feel that we will have accomplished our purpose in presenting this material to you. If you can use most of the techniques, we feel that you will be taking a big step forward towards making learning more effective for *students.*

Objectives

Figure 3.2 illustrates the four remaining parts of the workbook format—objectives, questions, references, and notes. These four parts are usually found on the same page, although some variation is possible, such as listing the objectives on a separate page or eliminating the note-taking space.

In this particular design format, each behavioral objective has been referenced directly across from the question(s) which will be used by the student to make a response. A direct relationship is sought, although the objectives could be listed together on a separate page. The overall attempt in this design format is one of assuring that the student is attending to the topic at hand and will know exactly what to anticipate. It was pointed out above that, in an ordinary lesson plan presentation, students generally have difficulty identifying critical content. By having an objective placed directly before him during the presentation, and cued by the teacher to the effect that a particular objective is the one under discussion, the student has a point of reference to which he can pay continued attention in terms of an expected behavioral outcome. It is the objective the student is to attend to, not the question(s). For organizational purposes, the student will find it of value to write his notes under the objectives to which they relate.

Questions

This section is provided to take care of the problem of active responding. It is the most important section of the workbook. Here the student can test his understanding of the instruction presented. He will test his "learning" of each objective to which he has been attending.

A task easier said than done is to get the students to use the workbook in the way it was designed to be used. This

Figure 3.2

Objectives	Objective-Questions	Ref.
1. Define "behavioral objective." NOTES:	1.1 Put an "X" beside each word that refers to an observable behavior; thus a word that might be used to state a behavioral objective. ....A. see ....C. identify ....E. understand ....G. appreciate ....B. hear ....D. explain ....F. list ....H. write	Mager 13-24
	1.2 Define the term "behavioral objective"..	Mager 3
2. Name the two principal uses of behavioral objectives within instruction. NOTES:	2.1 What are the two principal uses of behavioral objectives within instruction? (1) .... (2)	Det. Unit 9
	2.2 Since a behavioral objective specifies a behavioral........................, it is of direct value to both..............and.................in terms of what is to be learned from the process of instruction.	
3. List the two kinds of information obtained from the use of a pre-test. NOTES:	3.1 What are the two sources of information to be derived from the use of a pre-test given prior to instruction? (1) .... (2)	Det. Unit 9

generally found it to be a waste of space.

With the workbook format behind us as the student's interactive segment of an interactive lesson plan, let us now focus on the lesson plan itself and how it is related to accomplishing and directing the student to his interaction within the workbook.

Lesson Plan

There are five parts to the *lesson plan design*, as illustrated in Figure 3.3. Each part is associated with overcoming the problems outlined previously—namely, continuity of teacher presentation, and student problems associated with identifying critical content, active responding, and feedback. The five parts are:

Content Breakdown
Instructions
Objectives
Content Reminders
Responses and Feedback

Content Breakdown

As with any lesson plan design, the general topic of instruction is subdivided into content areas. This breakdown of content is determined not by the content itself but by the sequence of objectives. It is to the objectives that a content description of major and minor topics is assigned. The value lies in letting the students and teacher know that a general topic is to be presented as a point of reference, under which several objectives will be learned. It is an attempt to establish a continuity of instruction from class to class. Figure 3.3 is a content breakdown described by assignment number, titles, and descriptive phrases.

Figure 3.3

Assignment 2

LESSON PLAN **SOME TECHNIQUES FOR IMPROVING IN-CLASS EFFECTIVENESS**

I. PRE-CLASS ACTIVITIES

A. *Behavioral Objectives*

Note: Have students read Objectives 1 & 2.

Objective 1: Define "behavioral objective."

> What is learning? Content, or better—change in behavior.
> *EXERCISE*: Content, write acceptance of performance. Evaluate.
> *OVERHEAD No. 14*: Levels of Specificity: Goal, Objective, question—content.
>
> Q1.1C: (c) identify, (d) explain, (f) list, (h) write
>
> Objective—observable and measurable. Observable vs. indirectly observable.

Q1.2C: A statement in learner (student) terms which defines an observable, therefore measurable, behavioral outcome.

Objective 2: Name the two principal advantages to be derived from the use of behavioral objectives.

> Students—learning targets. Communicate a behavioral change.
> Teacher—planning and implementation.

Q2.1C: See above.
QS2.2 C: Outcome (intent), student and teacher.

B. *Pre-Tests*

Note: Have students read Objective 3.

Objective 3: List the two kinds of information obtained from the use of a Pre-Test.

> What is a Pre-test? Given: Before class or in class, prior to lecture.
> 1. Assumed prerequisites to course objectives.
> 2. Knowledge about course objectives. What student should attend to. Scan before class.

Instructions

Instructions give direction to the student as to what to attend to. Instructions are written in the lesson plan format as they come from the teacher to the students. They are written in the lesson plan because they *must* be given as instructions to the students. This is basically an attempt to deal with the problem of identifying critical content. In general, the word "note" has been used in this design format to indicate instructions.

Instructions include telling the student when to read objectives, the content of which will be presented thereafter. Instructions also include a range of other requirements, such as to read, view, or hear something prior to entering a presentation. It might be a reminder to the teacher to read the objective(s) to the class.

Objectives

The purpose of a lesson plan is to direct instruction, by a teacher, towards the objectives to be achieved by students. Since the students are attending to the objectives that are sequenced in their workbook, it is important that the teacher have the objectives before him as well. Listing the objectives in the lesson plan is the most critical requirement for getting at the problems of continuity and assuring that the presentation will fall within the critical content to be learned by the student. When both the student and teacher know that they are attending to the same objective, the teacher can keep directing the content presentation at the objective, and the student can work at the behavioral requirement of the objective. The problem is more readily understood if one thinks of a lesson plan without objectives, in which case the *teacher* may realize what direction is being taken, but *students* are without the benefit of knowing what kind of behavioral outcome is expected of them. In such a situation, about the only time the students find out what is expected of them is at test time—and that's a little too late.

Content Reminders

The rectangular boxes in Figure 3.3 are for content reminders. This section is the more usual part of any lesson plan. Essentially, it includes key reminders of content and illustrations to be used. It may also include other instructions not specifically described in the "note" (instructions) part of the design, for example, instructions as to "enabling" questions to be answered by students. "Enabling" questions will be discussed shortly.

When designing a lesson plan for your own use, this blocked-off section can be filled in. If, however, you are designing a lesson plan to be used by several other teachers, it is suggested that this space be left blank. This will allow the individual teacher to insert the content he needs as reminders and to use examples that he has found successful. It will be noted that the objectives, response demands, and confirmations remain the same, thus assuring continuity of critical content, but allowing for individual teacher differences in presentation of content.

Responses and Feedback

At appropriate points, the "structured" (questions in the workbook) interaction between what the teacher has said or shown and what the student is to perform must take place. Self-initiated, unstructured interaction, in the form of questions generated by students, should also continue to occur.

There does not necessarily have to be an interaction immediately after the presentation for each objective, but it is important that interaction occur sometime for every objective. The lesson plan may be so designed that two or more related objectives are presented; then a series of questions is asked. Whatever the sequence may be, the teacher should have written directions as to when the interaction is to occur. In Figure 3.3, points of interaction are indicated by a "Q" for question. For instance, questions 1.2, 2.1, and 2.2 should be asked in that order. These questions are in the student workbook. Following the question number is the letter "C," for confirmation—the answer to the question. The "QS" in front of question 2.2 means that this particular question is a summary question covering a series of previously responded-to questions.

There was mentioned under the topic of "content reminders" the need to provide enabling questions. You will note in Figure 3.3 that, in the blocked-off boxes, instructions appear for other questions (e.g., 1.1) and confirmations. These enabling questions are to be asked during instruction, as opposed to questions that are to be asked at the end of a block of instruction (e.g., 1.2). Such enabling questions are used to clarify certain aspects of the criterion question(s) which test the objective as a whole. For instance, question 1.1 clarifies some aspect of the terminal criterion question 1.2. Question 1.2 is itself the question used to test the objective. From the viewpoint of an instructional design format, this distinction in types of questions is mentioned only to point out that some questions appear within the content reminder part of the lesson plan, while other questions appear after the content reminders.

In terms of feedback, although the confirmation is written in the lesson plan, it need not necessarily come directly and always from the teacher. The confirmation can be elicited from students, or students could make use of flash cards for multiple-choice questions. The use of flash cards will be discussed in the next chapter.

In viewing the lesson plan format, in general, there are a number of variations both in the format and in what might be provided within the lesson plan. It might be desirable to place certain questions only within the lesson plan itself and not print them in the workbook. In this case, only the question number and space to answer that question would be provided in the workbook. The teacher would ask the question orally, in which case the question must be written in the lesson plan.

Instructions to work a set of problems in a textbook could be specified in the lesson plan, as well as many other variations. Whatever additional details are decided upon as requirements for either the lesson plan or the workbook, one should be guided by simplicity, and with constant attention to overcoming the problems related to designing an interactive lesson plan—continuity, attention to critical content, response needs, and feedback.

Outcomes Expected

Outcomes to be expected from the use of an *interactive* lesson plan are best assessed against what this instructional design achieves beyond that of an *ordinary* lesson plan.

It is the interactive component of the design that produces the favorable outcomes. For one, students become more actively involved in instruction. There is a built-in response orientation to instruction—that is, student responding is featured, rather than a stimulus-oriented form of instruction from the teacher. From the structured response demands in the workbook comes a more spontaneous form of interaction via questions generated by students themselves. Their own questions are more easily brought forth, because they seek further clarification to the structured responses in the workbook, and in part because they become more used to answering questions through use of the workbook itself. The overall outcome is more effective in-class instruction.

For the student, the problem of identifying critical

content is overcome to a high degree. Both the target of a behavioral outcome which he attends to as the teacher presents content and the response demands in the workbook function together in overcoming this problem.

The mere fact that objectives exist should make the student's note-taking easier to organize. Furthermore, he has some means of comparing his notes with the responses. The confirmation of responses will further verify the relevance of notes.

For the teacher, there is the assurance that all content deemed necessary to be covered *will be covered*. There is a built-in check on this. How? When such content is not presented, students will not be able to respond. Therefore, the teacher can reassess what critical content is still required in order to make the presentation complete. Anyone who has ever taught knows the feeling of frustration in not knowing if the students have "gotten it." Active, correct responding by students tells the teacher if they have "gotten it."

Of particular concern to the teacher is the recognition of which students have not been learning *what* material. An accurate assessment of this prior to final achievement testing is difficult to come by in the ordinary lesson plan. Both the workbook and the constant activity of in-class responding provide the accurate means against which to assess student problems prior to final testing. Such problems can then be taken care of by individual, one-to-one, teacher-to-student relationships and/or in-class and out-of-class branching to remedial forms of instruction (e.g., PI texts, etc.).

Finally, since it is primarily a teacher form of instructional design with which we are concerned, and in most instances such a design will be used for many class presentations, the continuity of effective instruction is much more easily assured. The objectives, responses, and feedback remain the same from one class to another. The treatment of content may vary, but the constant assessment of correct student responding must be ultimately achieved. In a sense, it is the students who will rightfully demand instruction that produces the outcome expected of them. The teacher is put on the spot by each individual in the class to produce effective instruction towards these outcomes.

CHAPTER IV

CONSTRUCT LESSON PLAN

Use

When you really think about it, most classroom instruction is rather inefficient. It often takes up a great deal of valuable student learning time with concepts and skills that students have *already learned* through the preparatory study assigned to them or that they know as part of their general background knowledge. The inefficiency referred to here should not be taken to mean that classroom instruction is unnecessary or that it does not in many instances contain a great deal of effectiveness (students learn) and efficiency (time it takes to learn). It is just that teachers assign a lot of preparatory work to students and then end up rehashing some or much of what was learned in preparatory study. This waste of time is rationalized away, and teachers go along with the practice of rehashing.

Put in the form of another rationalization, it is sometimes said that the task of the teacher is to put what the students have read into "perspective" so as to make sure the students have learned. Whatever rationalization it is put behind, it comes out as a waste of learning time.

Now, if we are honest with ourselves, in that we accept the premise that students do learn something prior to entering the classroom and that our task is not to rehash it, then we should investigate how to make our in-class instruction more efficient. The achievement of efficiency referred to is that of directing our in-class instructional time to *those learning objectives that the student really needs help with,* and not to those he has already learned by himself. The Construct Lesson Plan instructional design is one such means of assuring a higher degree of in-class efficiency of instruction. It certainly is not the only way, and other approaches have been suggested, such as individualized, self-paced, and student-controlled designs. But these are approaches for individuals, and if the intent is to provide "classroom" instruction, or you are just stuck with it, in the classical sense of a teacher providing the instruction to a group of students, then we are back to the kind of instructional design that can be used by a teacher. That is where the Construct Lesson Plan will find its use.

The use of a Construct Lesson Plan is for *classroom, group instruction.* However, it is *an attempt to individualize learning in the classroom environment.* It is presupposed that such group instruction is preceded by preparatory study on the part of students, possibly through use of one of the other instructional designs suggested in this text (e.g., Adjunct Study Guide) or at least some form of outside preparatory study (such as the more traditional reading assignments).

The emphasis given thus far to the Construct Lesson Plan has been that of dealing with learning efficiency. However, this is not the only problem of classroom instruction to which it is addressed. It is not necessary to go over again the other problems of instruction it helps to overcome, as such problems were adequately discussed in Chapter III in the description of the Interactive Lesson Plan. It is mentioned here only to emphasize that the Construct Lesson Plan is also concerned with those problems associated with the continuity of instruction, active student involvement, and feedback. You are referred to Chapter III for discussion of such problems and how they are overcome. Nevertheless, what the Construct Lesson Plan does deal with and solve that the Interactive Lesson Plan design does not is the added problem of learning efficiency. This efficiency problem is important; for, like effectiveness of instruction, it has some relationship to such concerns as maintaining student interest and avoiding boredom with things they have already learned. Finally, efficiency has a direct relationship to the dollars and cents of instruction.

Operational Description

The Construct Lesson Plan is literally a lesson plan that is "constructed" by the teacher to meet current student learning needs as those needs fall due when students enter the classroom. To say that the lesson plan is constructed means that it is not a predetermined plan for a lesson that will be implemented in the classroom. Rather, it is constructed in the classroom when valid data are collected and assessed about what the students have not learned in their preparatory study.

As it is used here in the operational description of the Construct Lesson Plan, to say that the lesson plan is "constructed" in its *entirety* in the classroom is only a half-truth. Certain learning activities are really determined prior to entering the classroom and constructed into the lesson plan in advance. Nevertheless, in the broad sense, it can still be said that the lesson plan is constructed to meet the immediate instructional needs of students. To be more specific, certain learning activities are preplanned and built into the lesson plan, while other learning activities are constructed at the time the teacher enters the classroom, and are based on finding out what the students presently do not know. In both instances the lesson plan is to be directed towards those objectives the students have yet to master, rather than all the objectives of a given lesson. The lesson plan *is* constructed to meet current learning needs.

Why then do we need to preplan for activities, and how do we construct the other learning activities that can only be determined when students enter the classroom? First, let us look at why preplanning is necessary and how it is accomplished in the direction of those objectives students have yet to master, or at least we think they have yet to master.

Even the most skilled teacher would feel rather apprehensive about entering a classroom without an idea of some learning activities that should be undertaken. This feeling itself is some justification for why preplanning is necessary. This need for preplanning stems from the valid concern that to go in unprepared might well result in a waste of valuable student learning time. Of course, this possible inefficiency is the very thing we are trying to avoid. However, within this concern, the teacher must realize that student preparatory study has or should have resulted in the students' entering the classroom with the ability to meet some of the objectives under study.

First, we need to think in terms of those objectives the students probably did not master, even though they studied these objectives in the preparatory study. If this can be done with a reasonable degree of accuracy, we at least go into the classroom with some planned learning activities. There are two areas within which such preplanning can be concentrated, each of which would not be in violation (at least within reason) of possible rehashing of what the student has already learned. This latter statement is made with the cautionary note that we may enter the classroom and find out otherwise—that the students do know what we have planned as a learning activity. The two preplanning areas are: (1) problem areas (objectives) of learning that we know about as a result of teaching experience or that continue to show up from an on-going validation process, and (2) areas (objectives) of learning that require added practice. Each of these will be discussed before turning to those learning activities that can only be assessed when the student actually enters the classroom.

Within almost any given lesson plan presentation, there seem to emerge certain objectives with which students have continued learning difficulties. Year after year these objectives keep coming up as the really hard objectives for students to master. The teacher often indicates this when he or she says, "You know, students just never seem to get this concept." Better yet, the problem areas are indicated by comments from students and achievement tests taken by the students. This is not to suggest that the exact problem area will arise year after year for the students for whom we are currently planning the lesson, but only that such problem areas are fairly good indicators of needed learning activity.

A more objective means of monitoring and realistically knowing what learning problems exist is to have an on-going course validation program. That is, when a lesson plan has been validated year after year by pre-post testing means, such tests usually indicate certain areas with which the students have continued difficulty. These are learning problems for which the teacher should be continually trying to find means to effectively communicate with the students. If problem areas exist, the teacher cannot simply ignore them. These continuing problem areas can be planned for by designing a new approach that might well overcome the problem area for the current students.

The second area we can prepare for and design into the Construct Lesson Plan prior to entering the classroom is that of providing needed practice. Certain objectives within a lesson often are of the kind that require added practice to sharpen the students' skill. Mathematics objectives are the more obvious illustration of this need. What we should do is isolate those objectives of the intended lesson that require added practice, and provide for such practice within the Construct Lesson Plan. In so doing, such activity can lead to an opportunity to check on individual student performance.

Now, what about those learning activities that can only be assessed and thus "constructed" into the Construct Lesson Plan when the students actually enter the classroom? Two indicators can be used to determine what the students need as learning activities.

One of the most immediate problems confronting the teacher with students sitting there before him or her in the classroom is that the teacher does not have a great deal of time to spend on assessing the current learning problems of students. Even if time did exist, could the teacher then build the learning activities into a lesson plan? Obviously the teacher cannot take thirty minutes of a one-hour classroom period of time to sit before the students and construct a lesson plan. At most, the teacher will have about five mintues to construct what is about to be described. As unattainable as it might seem at first, it can be done.

The task is to find out what objectives the students have not learned. When they walk in and the door is shut, you are suddenly faced with finding out what they know and what they do not know. What they do not know must be provided for, so that when the door is opened again they will know it, or at least have a greater chance of acquiring it on their own.

The first and most obvious thing is to ask the students what their problem areas (objectives) are. This is subjective information, but an indication nonetheless. It is an attempt to find what the class as a whole is having difficulty with. If it is a problem area for one or two students out of forty, then an evaluation of whether to cover it in class will have to be made by the teacher. Whatever is found as a problem area worth spending the time on must then be constructed into the lesson plan. And this includes providing the opportunity for the students to interact via constructed questions which can be given orally and to receive confirmation in the usual sense of providing interactive instruction. The problem area can be written down, with possible content reminders of what to say, with examples; and then other problem areas can be discussed. If students are given advance notice to come to class with their own problem areas written down, the assessment of such areas is made much easier. Furthermore, if such written questions by students are provided, say, one day in advance, some preparatory work outside of the classroom is then possible.

Written or oral questions given to the teacher still have some subjective overtones to them. For instance, the teacher may get some questions on problem areas from certain students who already have learned the objective(s) that they say are problem areas for them. They only want to hear it again to make sure they are right, which is not so bad, but it can be a waste of valuable in-class instructional time. Because student comments on their own problem areas are subjective, this leads to a discussion of a more objective means of assessing student problem areas at the point students enter the classroom.

The most objective means to assess student learning difficulties is to give a test. Is there enough time available in the classroom to give a test prior to instruction, then to construct a lesson plan around it, and then to give the lesson? The answer is "yes," but that "yes" depends upon how the test is constructed and the means used to evaluate the results of the test. In any case, if a test could be administered at the beginning of instruction, in a relatively short period of time, the most direct, objective indication of student learning difficulties would be indicated.

The quickest type of test to administer and score is a discrimination test—one containing multiple-choice, true-false, and matching questions. Some special words of caution must be given about such discrimination tests. First, the test items should not be simply selected from content in general. Rather, the test items should be written relative to all of the objectives of an assignment. Second, the discrimination questions should be true indicators of the behavior specified in the objectives—and here is where you can run into difficulties. For instance, suppose an objective called for the student to define a term. Given the term, he would write the definition. Would a multiple-choice question in which the student selects a definition from several possibilities be a true indicator of the objective which specifies that the student is to write the definition? Or, as another example, would a multiple-choice question be a true indicator of an objective calling for an explanation of a concept? The only reliable means for you to be sure that discrimination questions are equivalent to other verbal (i.e., describe, explain, list) questions and even possibly manipulative skills is through the process of validation. That is, during validation you could use both a discrimination question and verbal question when testing for a verbal objective, and reliably determine if the discrimination question measures the same performance on the verbal objective as would the verbal question itself. If so, the discrimination question can be said to be a reliable, equivalent indicator of performance for what is otherwise a verbal objective.

If these cautionary points can be adhered to, so that a valid test composed of discrimination items is drawn up, then a quick and ready means for objectively assessing current student knowledge about the objectives of a lesson is made possible. Still, the teacher is confronted with the time involved in test scoring, in the sense of finding out if the students are right or wrong. Since the teacher is in the classroom, he or she does not have an hour to score all the tests and plot the areas of difficulty to be included in the lesson plan. There is a way to overcome this time problem of scoring, however. This is done by using a type of flash card.

Flash cards are simply sets of different-colored cards wherein each color is used to indicate a different type of answer. For instance, if we gave each student cards of green, red, yellow, and blue, the colored cards might be used to indicate the following responses:*

GREEN	RED	YELLOW	BLUE
1	2	3	4
A	B	C	D
True	False		
Yes	No		

The teacher, in administering the discrimination test, then might ask the students as a group to answer questions by holding up the cards corresponding to what they believe the answers to be. The teacher then can easily assess the correctness or incorrectness relative to the colors of the cards. If, for example, the correct answer to a question is B, and all students hold up the red card, then performance for the class as a whole could be judged by the teacher as satisfactory. If, on the other hand, the correct answer to a question were C, and several of the students held up the green cards, then a direct indication of lack of satisfactory performance would be indicated on that objective, necessitating coverage in the Construct Lesson Plan.

While on the topic of testing prior to in-class instruc-

---

*The color should appear on only one side of the card so that the students cannot see one another's answers.

tion, you might well wonder why such a test could not be given to students prior to their entering the classroom. This would ease the time problem associated with completing the test in class. You could still have the students indicate their answers by means of the colored cards at the beginning of the class period. However, giving the test prior to entering the classroom brings up the problem of how accurate the results of the test would be. Students could have helped one another, and obviously have the benefit of resources to look up the answers. You will simply have to make a judgment for your own learning environment and students.

Operationally, then, the Construct Lesson Plan is a construct of (1) problem areas of student learning that continue to be problem areas time after time; (2) practice areas needing continued in-class practice; (3) problem areas as expressed by students; and (4) problem areas as shown by objective testing. Areas 1 and 2 can be written into the lesson plan prior to entering the classroom, and in that sense are not "constructed" into the lesson plan. However, areas 3 and 4 are assessed at that point when the teacher is confronted with the students at the beginning of a lesson and must therefore be "constructed" into the lesson plan.

Design Format

There are few unique aspects about the design format of a Construct Lesson Plan that have not already been discussed under that design entitled the Interactive Lesson Plan, Chapter III. Thus, all of the same essential components need not be described again.

The uniqueness of the Construct Lesson Plan is in the approach taken to what will constitute the instructional activities in the classroom. There are, however, two different arrangements in the physical layout of the design format that can be used to make "construction" and implementation of the Construct Lesson Plan easier.

The teacher has two options open regarding how to go about constructing the lesson plan. Either the teacher writes the problem areas down as they are expressed by students or indicated by testing and presents the lesson from memory; or the teacher must have a complete lesson plan already drawn up and *selects* those objectives and their related content reminders, questions, and so forth, that will be presented, based on student need. It is suggested that the latter approach be used, in that the former has the disadvantages of not having the continuity of instruction and built-in interaction that are more readily available in a lesson plan that is already written down. If teachers can construct and implement a lesson plan from memory, then more power to them, but be wary of any sacrifices made in interaction with students. Let us look at the option of a prepared lesson plan; how it differs from any other lesson plan format; and how it can be used to construct a lesson plan for current student learning needs.

Because the teacher will not know prior to entering the classroom what specific objectives will be the focus of instruction, other than those which were described as continuing problem and practice areas, some means of flexibility in the layout, particularly the sequence, of the lesson plan must exist. This flexibility should allow the teacher to easily find that part of the lesson plan which will deal only with the objectives of the testing and student problem areas that have been found to need instruction. To illustrate, the overall lesson might well involve some fifteen objectives. Of these, based on testing and direct indication from students about problem areas of concern to them, it is found that the students need some instructional assistance on three particular objectives. Rather than "rummaging" through an Interactive Lesson Plan, and having the students do likewise in their workbooks, it would be easier to arrange the instruction for each objective on separate cards and the questions for students on separate cards. What are these cards?

Figure 4.1 illustrates, again, the lesson plan design for the Interactive Lesson Plan in Chapter III. Note that the design has more than one objective to a page, with its associated content reminders, confirmations, and so forth. Note also that some objectives have been grouped together for instruction, such as objectives 1 and 2. The "card" arrangement referred to above would physically arrange the objectives and associated instruction separately. For example, Figure 4.2 illustrates two separate cards for the same objectives 1 and 2 in Figure 4.1. Thus, if the students had already mastered objective 1, as indicated by the testing prior to beginning instruction, then the teacher would simply remove the card with objective 2 and place it before him or her. Other cards, each dealing with separate objectives, could in the same manner be taken from the stack of lesson plan cards. Again, selection is based upon the need for use as determined by testing, student request, and/or those continuing problem areas selected before class time.

What has been given above is simply a difference in the physical arrangement of the lesson plan. The same basic components are used for the Construct Lesson Plan as for the Interactive Lesson Plan; the difference is that the objectives and their associated instructional activities are placed on separate cards. But, this is only part of the total lesson plan.

It was mentioned that there is another difference in the Construct Lesson Plan. This difference relates to the need to have some blank cards, such as in Figure 4.3. The teacher will find in the implementation of the Construct Lesson Plan that these blank cards are useful in two ways. One, since some of the lesson plan may be based on providing added practice, the blank cards are useful for specifying what that practice will be. What one particular classroom full of students needs as added practice may not be the same as for another. In addition, an existing lesson plan itself does not usually contain enough practice problems, and there is a need to develop others. The blank cards can be used for this purpose.

A second use to be made of the blank cards is in regard to those instances in which it is found, either by testing or student questions, that what the student needs help with is not a whole objective but some *part* of it. For instance, suppose an objective specifies that the student will explain four particular concepts. The students indicate at the beginning of the class that what they do not exactly understand is concept number 2. The teacher could easily write this concept needing attention on the blank card and arrange it with other cards that will make up the total lesson. Incidentally, this card will be of value after the lesson, for it probably indicates some revision that is needed in the lesson plan itself.

What has been described here as a design format for a Construct Lesson Plan is an individual-objective, with associated instruction, card arrangement. Such a card arrangement allows the teacher to easily select, write, and sequence cards that will form the "constructed" lesson plan to meet existing instructional needs of students in the classroom. As a final reminder, it should be noted that the Construct Lesson Plan is an instructional design that is used in conjunction with some other instructional design (i.e., Adjunct Study Guide) that mediates instruction outside the classroom, prior to in-class instruction. The Construct Lesson Plan then provides a convenient, effective, and *efficient* way of conducting in-class instruction towards those objectives not achieved outside the classroom. Its most salient characteristic is that it is a way to provide instruction in the *immediate*, up-to-date learning requirements of the students.

Figure 4.1

LESSON PLAN   **SOME TECHNIQUES FOR IMPROVING IN-CLASS EFFECTIVENESS**

I.   PRE-CLASS ACTIVITIES

A.   *Behavioral Objectives*

Note: Have students read Objectives 1 & 2.

Objective 1: Define "behavioral objective."

> What is learning? Content, or better—change in behavior.
> *EXERCISE*: Content, write acceptance of performance. Evaluate.
> *OVERHEAD No. 14*: Levels of Specificity: Goal, Objective, question—content.
>
> Q1.1C: (c) identify,   (d) explain,   (f) list,   (h) write
>
> Objective—observable and measurable. Observable vs. indirectly observable.

Q1.2C: A statement in learner (student) terms which defines an observable, therefore measurable, behavioral outcome.

Objective 2: Name the two principal advantages to be derived from the use of behavioral objectives.

> Students—learning targets. Communicate a behavioral change.
> Teacher—planning and implementation.

Q2.1C: See above.
QS2.2 C: Outcome (intent), student and teacher.

B.   *Pre-Tests*

Note: Have students read Objective 3.

Objective 3: List the two kinds of information obtained from the use of a Pre-Test.

> What is a Pre-test? Given: Before class or in class, prior to lecture.
>   1.   Assumed prerequisites to course objectives.
>   2.   Knowledge about course objectives. What student should attend to. Scan before class.

Figure 4.2

Card 2-1

LESSON PLAN SOME TECHNIQUES FOR IMPROVING
IN-CLASS EFFECTIVENESS

I. PRE-CLASS ACTIVITIES

A. *Behavioral Objectives*

Note: Have students read Objective I.

Objective 1: Define "behavioral objective."

> What is learning? Content, or better—change in behavior.
> *EXERCISE*: Content, write acceptance of performance. Evaluate.
> *OVERHEAD No. 14*: Levels of Specificity: Goal, Objective,
> question—content.
>
> Q1.1 C: (c) identify, (d) explain, (f) list, (h) write
>
> Objective—observable and measurable. Observable vs. indirectly
> observable.

Q1.2 C: A statement in learner (student) terms which
defines an observable, therefore measurable, behavioral outcome.

Card 2-2

Assignment 2

LESSON PLAN SOME TECHNIQUES FOR IMPROVING
IN-CLASS EFFECTIVENESS

I. PRE-CLASS ACTIVITIES

A. *Behavioral Objectives*

Note: Have students read Objective 2.

Objective 2: Name the two principal advantages to be derived from the
use of behavioral objectives.

> Students—learning targets. Communicate a behavioral change.
> Teacher—planning and implementation.

Q2.1 C: See above

QS2.2 C: Outcome (intent), student and teacher.

Figure 4.3

```
                                    Card ...........
                   Assignment ...........

    LESSON PLAN  .....................................................................
        TOPIC       ...................................|....
        A.    Sub-Topic   ...........................................
              Note:  Read Objectives ........... to students
              Objective      ...............   ..........................................
                    ┌────────────────────────────────────────┐
                    │                                          │
                    │                                          │
                    └────────────────────────────────────────┘
                         Question ...........
```

Outcomes Expected

Outcomes from the use of the Construct Lesson Plan are *the same* as those discussed for the Interactive Lesson Plan in Chapter III.

The intent in utilizing the Construct Lesson Plan approach to classroom instruction is basically to produce a lesson to meet *current* student learning requirements. Since the requirements are based on what the students need as instruction rather than on what they already know, efficiency of instruction is improved. And, because there is efficiency, students are not bored with instruction covering what they already know. Their interest in what is being presented should be greater, not only because the lesson is concerned with what they do not know, but also because they have actually had a hand in constructing the lesson plan. They make an input both by their own questions needing clarification and by the results of pre-testing.

CHAPTER V

ADJUNCT STUDY GUIDE

Use

The Adjunct Study Guide is most useful in meeting an instructional requirement in which there is complete independent student study or a high percentage of independent study with some group classroom time. It is also useful when it is necessary, whether for financial or other reasons, that *existing* instructional materials be utilized.

An Adjunct Study Guide is an instructional design that uses existing instructional or informational resources as the key sources of content, while the guidance through and interaction with such items are provided by the format of the study guide. A definition of study guide must necessitate the use of the terms themselves, meaning a guide that directs student study. An *Adjunct* Study Guide means a guide to instruction that does not contain all or possibly any of the content within it, but rather *relies on external sources for the content of instruction.* Therefore, it does not attempt to put all instructional materials physically together in one package, but utilizes a variety of instructional materials that already exist. The study guide is then a "map" that guides the student through the content material. Any deficiencies in these materials—for instance, content areas that are found to be ineffective—are made up for by writing *new* and effective materials to be included physically within the study guide or as materials to be referenced by the study guide, but *located elsewhere.*

Existing instructional materials generally lack an interactive component, requiring student responding during content presentation. Almost any textbook will indicate this deficiency of interaction. Also, there is a general lack of confirmation to such responding and direction as to what "critical" content is to be learned by the student. An Adjunct Study Guide takes care of these deficiencies by guiding the student to the critical content and by providing the missing interaction that he needs. By definition, then, an Adjunct Study Guide is an instructional design that provides the direction through and interaction with existing content in sources made available to students as learning resources.

An Adjunct Study Guide has two principal uses: (1) as a means of independent study, and (2) as a means of independent study to be augmented by other instruction, such as in-class instruction. For reasons that shortly will be explained, it is suggested that in approaching the development of an Adjunct Study Guide, the designer think in terms of its use as if it were to be employed solely for independent study—that it will not be augmented by in-class instruction. To understand why this approach to development is suggested, one must understand both the learning environment in which students are normally placed and certain motivational aspects behind their study.

First, an understanding of the student's learning environment is important, for it tells us something about the *degree* of instruction that must be provided. The following will serve as a general description of the environment in which we usually find students.

Visualize the student as a lonely character, somewhere "out there" on his own, about to enter a classroom. If, as teachers or designers of instruction, we assume that student study outside of a classroom is less important than what occurs inside the classroom (or, put another way, that we will take care of what he does not learn outside, inside the classroom), then we are sacrificing both some learning effectiveness and efficiency for ourselves as teachers and for the students as learners. What typically happens in classroom instruction is that we say to the student, "You read or do this outside of class and then come to class and I'll go over the whole thing with you again." We assume, in a sense, that students cannot learn all or at least much of what we want them to learn, outside of the classroom; or, if we assume they can learn outside, we do very little about it. If, on the other hand, we did assume and *validate* certain assumptions—that they could and do learn outside the classroom—then the small amount of valuable time for in-class activity could be devoted to more crucial requirements. Some of this in-class time could be devoted to behavioral objectives the students have not achieved outside the classroom. What we might do is assess by pre-test means what they did not learn on the outside as a group or individually, and work with them in the classroom as a group or as individuals.

The important point to be drawn from the discussion above is that if the study guide instructional design is chosen as a means to prescribe instruction, then, in developing that study guide, assume that you will try to teach "everything" through use of the study guide, whether or not it is to be augmented by classroom instruction. Assume that the student, in using a study guide, is not going to come to class. If he is going to come to class, then use the classroom time, which in reality is rather a short period of time, for purposes for which it is best suited. The classroom is most likely the only opportunity for the individual student to come and solve his *individual problems* with content he is attempting to master.

Why development should be viewed in this manner, as if we are serving the independent learner, can be further emphasized by looking also at student motivation towards study outside the classroom. If the students realize that no matter whether or not they read and learn the material outside the classroom, it will be rehashed again in class, then many of them do not feel any motivation to study outside the classroom. They draw the conclusion that they will "just take good notes *in class.*"

Obviously, there is a value in students coming together to share ideas, interpretations of content, and so forth. It is not being suggested here in any way that this activity be diminished or that it could be taken care of solely by independent study, using a study guide. Quite the contrary, what is being stressed is that "effective" study-guide learning can and will increase the potential of students to participate within the classroom. If students come to the classroom more fully versed in content, group activity is likely to occur on a higher and more desirable level. The Adjunct Study Guide is an instructional design in which the maximum of independent study can be realized, whether augmented by subsequent classroom instruction or not. When a study guide is to be developed, it should be produced on the assumption that it will be used for complete, independent study, without benefit of subsequent classroom instruction. In this way, if classroom instruction is to follow, such instruction will be more effective and efficient.

Operational Description

Since the Adjunct Study Guide is for student use, a student viewpoint should be taken in describing how this design works. The following features are provided:

1. *Instruction is provided according to behavioral objectives.* While a sequence is given, there is the possibility for

students to use the design in much the same way as in the case of the Learner Controlled Instruction design. That is, the students could have an option to study objectives according to their own interests and in almost any order. Also, the student can select and utilize sources of information according to what he needs.

2. *Since this is an "Adjunct" Study Guide, sources of existing instructional and informational material are required.* The range of possibilities is great. Existing texts, films, operational manuals, people, library materials, and so forth can be used. These are the sources of content the student will make use of, guided always by the directions in the study guide itself as to where and how much to read, view, or hear. When such sources are lacking (which is highly unlikely) or existing sources are inadequate or ineffective (which is more likely), sources of content may include some content written into the study guide itself.

3. *A means of structured interaction is provided, so that the student can assess if he is learning.* Interaction is provided by a series of questions or tasks related to the requirements spelled out in the behavioral objectives.

4. *A means of confirmation to the interaction is provided, so that students will know the correctness or incorrectness of their responses.* This is explained as part of the discussion which follows under the "Summary" sub-heading.

An Adjunct Study Guide works in this manner:

First, the student is given a set of behavioral objectives. Picture again the student as a lonely individual somewhere out in the world, on his own, studying assigned material that may or may not be augmented by in-class instruction. This mental picture should tell us that there is a need for *clear* direction to what is to be learned and exactly how the student will demonstrate what he learns. The designer of this instruction must communicate instructional intent as precisely as possible. This independent studier will be given a set of objectives as targets to be achieved and a large volume of materials that he must study in order to hit these targets. The targets must be clear and easily assessed as having been reached. This emphasis on the "lonely" student is intended to stress that the many features of what constitutes effective interactive instruction (Chapter I), including objectives, must be sought after in the study-guide approach to a higher degree than is the case with many other forms of instructional design.

Next, the student is given the existing instructional materials and information that present the content leading to the objectives. This is not meant to be so general as to say, "Here is a book; now go to it." Existing sources generally have a lot of unnecessary information in them that waste valuable study time. Also, such sources are not always clearly organized, so that the student can easily find what is to be studied. Therefore, in an Adjunct Study Guide, precise directions are given as to where to read and how much to study. For example, rather than specifying that the student will read Chapter I, it would be much better to specify pages 18 to 21 of Chapter I, excluding any discussion that relates to the topic of such-and-such. It may sound as if the intent is to overly guide the student by the fingernail, rather than by the whole hand, but there is not much sense in having him go through material that is not relevant, or having him spend time wading through that which only wastes his time. Thus far, then, the student has a set of objectives and specific references to content as the first two requirements of an Adjunct Study Guide.

Next is the provision for interaction that is generally lacking in content sources. To take care of this lack of interaction, the study guide contains specific questions and tasks relative to the objectives. The student reads an objective, studies the sources of content, and then interacts with questions.

What should then follow, of course, is confirmation as to the correctness or incorrectness of the student's responses (No. 4 above). This confirmation feature can best be described by looking at the design format itself.

Design Format

There are five sections to an Adjunct Study Guide. They are:

Purpose and Significance
Objectives
Objective-Questions
Summary
Cumulative Problem

Each will be described separately, with a discussion of how each relates to the others.

Purpose and Significance

The Purpose and Significance section is a description of *why* the student should study the material in a particular assignment or lesson. It is important to give the student an appreciation and motivation for studying. The Purpose and Significance is generally a one-page-or-less description of what the lesson is about and why it is important in relation to its eventual use or study in the first place. Figure 5.1 illustrates a Purpose and Significance section of an Adjunct Study Guide for a basic insurance course. What should be noted about the Purpose and Significance is that, first, it is a general descriptive statement about what content is going to be learned. Secondly, this statement is then followed by

Figure 5.1

PURPOSE AND SIGNIFICANCE

The life insurance policy has been characterized as a bundle of rights. In this assignment the student will review the basic whole life insurance policy as well as some of the fundamental legal principles which apply to those provisions. A greater appreciation of the utility and the adaptability of the life insurance contract thus will be secured. Goals to achieve include:

1. The life insurance agent will understand how each policy provision protects the rights of the insured in regard to an insurance policy.

2. The life insurance agent will be familiar with the broad range of benefits that are part of a life insurance contract.

3. The life insurance agent will know the characteristics of his product so that he can explain it to his clients and answer their questions.

Text Reference

Greider, J.E., and Beadles, W.T. *Law and the Life Insurance Contract.*

Figure 5.2

OBJECTIVES

When you have completed this assignment, you will be able to:

1. Explain what contract of "adhesion" means in relation to an insurance contract.
2. List the general information usually found on the FACE page of a basic whole life insurance policy.
3. Explain what "comply in substance" means as part of a statute setting forth required policy provisions.
4. In terms of specified conditions, explain the operation of each of the following STANDARD PROVISIONS found in an insurance policy:

   (1) Entire Contract Provision (5) Divisible Surplus
   (2) Incontestable Clause (6) Nonforfeiture Values
   (3) Grace Period (7) Policy Provision
   (4) Misstatement of Age (8) Reinstatement Clause

5. Explain the method of payment and limitations upon each of the following basic types of OPTIONAL SETTLEMENTS:

   (1) Interest Option
   (2) Fixed Period Option
   (3) Fixed Amount Option
   (4) Life Income

generic goals of what the student will understand, become familiar with, appreciate, or eventually know. These are goals and not behavioral objectives. In essence, the statement and goals together give a general picture of what is to be learned and why it should be learned.

Objectives

Section II, Objectives, is a listing of behaviorally stated objectives for the lesson. As an extension to the "Purpose and Significance," the student is instructed to read the set of objectives before proceeding into the reading materials, and to continue to use the objectives in conjunction with Section III, which will be discussed shortly. Figure 5.2 illustrates a set of objectives for the basic insurance course. These objectives are usually on a separate page or on the back of Section I, Purpose and Significance, as they need to be eventually removed for use with Section III. The behavioral objectives are a direct extension of the Purpose and Significance goals, as the achievement of the objectives will lead to satisfying the goals.

Objective-Questions

Section III, Objective-Questions, is divided into three parts: References, Objective-Questions, and Notes (see Figure 5.3).

Having read the Purpose and Significance (Section I) and the Objectives (Section II), the student proceeds through Section III as follows:

1. Beginning in the left column, the student notes a reference to read, or a direction to view a film, watch a performance task, etc. In the illustration given, G & B is a textbook with certain pages to read. In certain instances it might include what the

Figure 5.3

REF.   OBJECTIVE-QUESTIONS

Read Obj. 1-3   1a. Which of the following statements describe(s)
   G & B   a life insurance contract:
   174-
   175   .....a. informal   .....d. unilateral
   (exclude   .....b. aleatory   .....e. adhesion
   Pars. 1-3)   .....c. commutative   .....f. bargaining
                                                          contract

Answer
   a, b, d, e

1b. What does contract of "adhesion" mean in relation to an insurance contract?

Summary Item #1

   G & B   2. List the general information usually found on
   178   the FACE page of a basic whole life insurance policy.

Summary Item #2

   G & B   3. What does "comply in substance" mean as
   176 &   part of a statute setting forth required policy
   179   provisions?

Summary Item #3

student should not pay attention to.

2. The student reads the reference or references.

3. Having finished reading the content, he then answers a question or series of questions related to an objective. For example, in the illustration, he answers questions 1a and 1b related to objective 1 (in Section II).

4. He is given a confirmation of the question he just answered. With some exceptions, the confirmation is not found on the same page, directly after the question, as is the usual case in many interactive instructional designs, or as in programmed instruction texts. Rather the confirmation appears most often in what is called the Summary, Section IV. (The nature of exceptions will be elaborated upon in the discussion of Section IV.)

5. The student then goes to the next reference and repeats the cycle of steps 1 through 4. Notes can be added, as the student prefers.

Note in Section III that all references are to existing instructional materials. Also, such references may be given in an order according to the sequence of the objectives, and not necessarily in the order that the content appears in the reference itself. For example, in Figure 5.3, the reference G & B begins with pages 174-175, then goes to page 178, and back to page 176. This allows a sequence *according to objectives*, rather than to content dictated by how it appears in a textbook.

What Figure 5.3 does not illustrate is what you can do in the case of an objective for which you do not have an existing reference or for which the existing reference is ineffective for student learning. There is nothing to preclude writing your own material in the study guide or writing it as a separate segment and making reference to it. Good validation procedures should indicate when and where ineffective references exist. The time saved in utilizing existing materials that you *know* work, through validation, augmented by development of your own materials, should clearly speak for the cost-savings benefit in utilizing an adjunctive instructional design.

Before moving on to a discussion of Section IV, it should be pointed out that, as another format consideration, Sections II and III, as previously stated, can be combined into one integrated section. Certain advantages are to be gained in doing so, depending on the nature of the objectives and content. Figure 5.4 illustrates an example of combining an objective with the reference, notes, and questions.

The advantages to be gained by the format in Figure 5.4 are: (1) the objective is integrated directly with the reference source and questions; (2) the answer to a question is located so that it is less likely to be seen accidentally by the student; (3) the student need not flip from one section (II) to another (III), and thus administratively the format is easier for the student to use; and (4) a series of questions can be answered before the confirmation is given.

Summary

Section IV of the Adjunct Study Guide, the Summary, serves two unique functions. First, the Summary provides the confirmation function for the questions answered in Section III. In Figure 5.5, the confirmations for questions 2 and 3 (from Section III) are illustrated.

Confirmations are blocked off and numbered in the Summary to the corresponding questions in Section III, so that the student can find the confirmation with ease. Once he has confirmed a response, he then proceeds to the next reference in Section III; reads it; answers the question(s);

Figure 5.4

Objective   Explain what contract of "adhesion" means in relation to an insurance contract.

Reference   G&B pages 174-175 (Exclude first three paragraphs).

Notes

Questions   Which of the following statements describe(s) a life insurance contract:

.....a.	informal	.....d.	unilateral
.....b.	aleatory	.....e.	adhesion
.....c.	commutative	.....f.	bargaining contract

What does contract of "adhesion" mean in relation to an insurance contract?

Answers   a, b, d, e
Check Summary Item #1.

Figure 5.5

SUMMARY

The Policy in General

For ease of discussion, it is helpful to break the life insurance policy down into large general sections. Thus, the section dealing with beneficiary designations may be termed the settlement section; the nonforfeiture section specifies rights and privileges available if the policyowner discontinues premium payment before the policy becomes paid up; and a number of general provisions may be grouped in a third section. In addition, there is a face page, and there may be other benefits provided by additional sections or riders.

The Face Page

2   A common statutory provision requires a brief description of the coverage to be included on the face page of the life insurance contract. In addition to this, the face page usually includes a statement of the company's promise to pay the face amount to the beneficiary on receipt of due proof of the death of the insured and a statement of the premium payable. The testimonium or attestation clause consists of the execution paragraph and includes the signature of company officers—usually the president and secretary. The remainder of the policy defines this basic promise in more detail and explains the various rights and privileges of the owner.

The Standard Provisions

3   The standard provisions law lists a number of provisions that must be included in a life insurance policy form before it will be approved, but the company is not required to include these provisions in the exact words of the statute. It is sufficient if they comply with the statutory provision "in substance," e.g., that the words used be as favorable or more favorable to the policyholder than those required by the standard provision. Compliance is determined by the Commissioner of Insurance.

checks the confirmation in the Summary, and so on. Note that only the confirmations in the Summary are blocked off.

Once all questions have been answered and the lesson is completed, the second function of the Summary becomes evident, and that is as a "summary." By reading the Summary after completing the assignment, having answered all questions in Section III, the student can then tie together all previous responses. It is a summary of terminal objectives. This feature is particularly valuable with material that is cumulative in nature.

There are some important points to be understood about what goes into and what should be excluded from the Summary:

1. The Summary is a summary of responses to terminal objectives, that is, end-of-the-course objectives. Background information, or what are often called "enabling" objectives that aid in progressing towards successful performance of terminal objectives, and which also require responding via questions in Section III, is not confirmed in the Summary. Rather, such confirmation to background information is placed directly after the questions in Section III. Question 1a in Figure 5.3 is one such example of background information, the confirmation to which is provided directly after the question. The terminal question (1b) related to objective 1 in Section II *is* confirmed in the Summary. A simple word designation is used to direct the student to the proper location of the confirmation:

   Answer: appears in the study guide right after the question.

Summary Item No.: appears in Section IV, the
Summary.

The rationale applied to the Summary is that it is a
"summary" and should therefore summarize only
terminal objectives.

2.   A second point to raise about the Summary
     Section is how to provide a confirmation for
     discrimination objectives (those requiring responses
     by multiple-choice, matching, etc., as opposed to
     verbal objectives requiring constructed responses)
     within a summary. Confirmation of discrimination
     questions can be provided in a verbally constructed
     manner, i.e., the correct answer may be selection *d*
     out of choices *a, b, c, d,* and *e.* The confirmation
     would not appear in the Summary as just *d,* but
     with the word explanation of what *d* stands for.

3.   Note in the sample Summary that certain informa-
     tion is not blocked off; thus it is not part of some
     confirmation. This "information" is "connecting
     tissue," so to speak, as it links confirmations to
     make a summary out of the series of confirma-
     tions. It is important to note that any information,
     outside a blocked-off area, is only information, and
     cannot be instructional content which the student
     is expected to perform as an objective, unless, of
     course, it was previously responded to. It is the
     "nice-to-know" enrichment materials, but not
     material that is part of an objective (again, unless
     previously learned). In essence, summary confirma-
     tions (in the blocked-off areas) are what he *must*
     know, while the other is simply information.

Cumulative Problem

Section V, Cumulative Problem, is an optional section that the designer may or may not want to include with the Adjunct Study Guide. It has a function similar to that of the Summary section, as a "summary." Often the objectives achieved in an assignment need to be or can be brought together for application to a common problem or series of problems. Figure 5.6 illustrates a problem that calls for application of several of the objectives learned in the assignment. Other examples might include a chemistry course lesson in which the cumulative objectives lead to an experiment, or a spelling improvement lesson on doubling final consonants before adding suffixes that culminates in their application within sentences. Task-oriented lessons are common instances in which cumulative problems can be employed.

Figure 5.6

COURSE 2   POLICY PROVISIONS   SECTION V
ASSIGNMENT 3   PAGE 1

CUMULATIVE PROBLEM

(a) "Fundamental to the legality of any life insurance contract is the existence of an insurable interest."
    (1) Describe what is meant by an insurable interest.
    (2) Indicate when the insurable interest must be present in order for a life insurance contract to be enforceable.
    (3) Explain why the existence of an insurable interest is "fundamental to the legality of any life insurance contract."

(b) If in the following cases the question of insurable interest is raised, indicate, with reasons, whether the beneficiary could collect the proceeds of the contract and, if so, to what extent.

    (1) "A" purchases a life insurance contract on his life and designates his fiancee, "B," as beneficiary. "A" dies prior to their marriage.
    (2) "M" purchases a life insurance contract on the life of his son, "P," aged 10, and designates himself as beneficiary. "P" dies two years later.

(For Answer, See page 2)

A second, common function of the cumulative problem is to provide practice analogous to the final examination. The student may well be expected to pass an achievement test for the entire course, and the cumulative problems in a series of lessons provide an excellent way to provide periodic checks on learning before a final examination.

The cumulative problem is formulated to encompass as many as possible of the various aspects of the objectives learned in an assignment. These aspects of the objectives may be formulated on a generic or specific basis. Confirmations and explanations (not illustrated in Figure 5.6) of the cumulative problem are given immediately after the problem, by a sample answer or checklist, and might include specific references in the answer to objectives covered.

In summarizing the five sections of an Adjunct Study Guide, the student enters at a generic level (Purpose and Significance) to gain an overall idea of what is to be learned and why that learning is important. Specific learning requirements (Objectives) are then given to the student as a logical extension in detail of the Purpose and Significance. Entry into the content of a lesson is through the Objective-Question section, wherein specific reference is given to existing resources that can be utilized. This is followed by the opportunity to interact with the content (which normally, outside this design, lacks an interactive component) to check and practice what has been learned. The correctness of a response is given by immediate confirmation found in Section IV, the Summary. Not only is direct confirmation provided, but the means exist to tie confirmations together by use of the Summary section as a "summary." Finally, if applicable, a cumulative problem or series of problems is provided for purposes of combining objectives or as practice analogous to a final examination.

Outcomes Expected

As with any instructional design, outcomes to be expected should be viewed first in terms of what the design does for the student. The emphasis in discussing the Adjunct Study Guide is on use by the independent learner, and this emphasis should give some indication of what outcomes can be expected:

1. A much higher degree of both learning effectiveness and efficiency should be achieved. Because most existing instructional materials, particularly textbooks, are noninteractive, learning effectiveness is not as great as it should be. The Adjunct Study Guide provides the necessary interaction, through active responding and confirmation. In addition, behavioral objectives pinpoint the learning targets more clearly for students, so that they can aim their reading, viewing, or listening at the *critical* content. Learning efficiency is achieved because specific references can be given to content, thus avoiding unnecessary or totally irrelevant content. When ineffective or deficient existing materials are found, they can be replaced by adding new materials to the study guide. Designers and teachers are often confronted with existing sources of instructional materials that do not quite match the students' instructional needs, but do contain the bulk of content, and thus the ineffective material is "put up with." An adjunctive approach eases this problem.

2. A second outcome to be expected is that, once the objectives of a lesson are achieved, they will be "seen" in context. The lesson is not learned as a set of isolated objectives. Rather, through that part of the Adjunct Study Guide design known as the Summary, provisions are made to review the individual objectives in relation to one another. As pointed out above, this summary provision is particularly valuable with content that is cumulative in nature. In addition, students find the Summary quite valuable for

review purposes after initial learning.

3. If the development of an Adjunct Study Guide is approached from the standpoint that its use will be by the independent studier, regardless of whether or not it will be augmented by subsequent in-class instruction, then a higher level of student preparation for in-class instruction can be expected. Therefore, classroom instruction becomes a time for meeting special learning problems. But: "Will the students actually do the work outside class time?" The question is easier to answer for college level study or job training programs than, say, for high school students. That is obvious and true enough. But, consider, if students know they have to use the study guide because that is the way you designed the course; if they know it is *not* all going to be rehashed in class; if they know that such instruction is effective and efficient for them—then the study guide will be used by students. A good case can be made for the point of view that the reason students do not study outside class is not that they are lazy, but that they are given excuses not to study—and that the material given them lacks direction, objectives, and a real knowledge of "Am I learning?" An effective Adjunct Study Guide approach can take care of these doubts and problems.

4. Finally, a real cost savings can be expected in terms of development and use costs. Existing instructional materials constitute the bulk, if indeed not all, of the content.

CHAPTER VI

CORE PACKAGE

Use

It has been a concern in education that various courses of instruction, while defined as specific disciplines and organized into classroom schedules as such, should be viewed by students as generally having some relationship to one another. Hopefully, specific skills or concepts learned in one subject matter area will have a reinforcing effect of providing building blocks as necessary background knowledge to other subject matter areas. For instance, the study of chemistry might lead to applications in mathematics or to more generic concepts, such as general reasoning skills. In courses which are more training oriented, the attempt might be to relate such areas as math and science concepts learned elsewhere to job-oriented skills being learned in the training course itself. This is particularly true in basic training courses, where the trainee lacks basic fundamentals of math or reading. One way to emphasize a relationship between a primary course of study and peripheral courses of study is through the use of a Core Package.

What the title of this instructional design implies is that some subject matter area or skill training course will be the nucleus of instruction, called the core. Around this core, other disciplines will be built to help reinforce the core in some way. Reinforcement is generally for the purpose of showing that the core has relevance to other areas of study that are undertaken. The title Core Package may be somewhat misleading in that the instruction is not just a package of instruction for a single core, but rather includes other disciplines of instruction that relate to the central core. Also, "Core Package" has nothing whatever to do with the "Core Curriculum" concept which was once popular in some elementary and secondary schools, in reference to the teaching of English and social studies. Exactly why a Core Package approach to instruction is needed can be readily understood when seen from a student-need-and-use point of view towards learning in general.

One of our strongest indicators of a learning need or problem is what students say about a learning experience in which they are currently engaged. They might say:

> *"What does this course have to do with my getting a job?"*
> *"What does this course have to do with my other courses?"*
> *"Why study this stuff anyway?"*
> *"I really like course such and such, but I can't see what this course has to do with anything else!"*
> *"This course is a waste of my time!"*

There is a central theme in the comments above. That is, the students are expressing a need for something which will exhibit *relevance* between what they are presently learning and what they already know, or are currently learning in other courses, or what they might be doing in the future. Note carefully that the emphasis on relevance is not in the realm of the relevance of subject matter or skills to one another within a given course, but *between* courses, concepts already known, or some future events.

The Core Package can be used for either group or individual instruction, although it is normally used for individualized learning programs. How it is used depends on the degree to which content and interaction are specified in the various parts of the package, and the degree to which it is possible for teachers to administratively work together in implementing the "core" and its related instruction. "Working together" means that areas of study surrounding the core of instruction can be administered by teachers who work in concert with one another in the learning efforts of students they have in common. If the learning environment is such that teachers cannot work closely, then a more individually oriented, student self-administered program must be structured, and this includes the design aspects of the Core Package itself.

There probably is not a course or training program that could not, to one degree or another, use a Core Package design. This is not to suggest that existing, already effective courses be changed or that an existing or to-be-produced course should use the Core Package design *in toto. When and where there is a need for students to directly see and practice the relevance of one or more concepts that relate to the principal course under study, so as to reinforce the relevance of that course, the Core Package can have application.*

Operational Description

The Core Package instructional design contains behavioral objectives that serve three different learning functions. These functions are labeled as terminal, enabling, and relevancy objectives. Whatever skills or content the students are to learn, which is the primary reason for providing the instruction in the first place, are specified as the terminal objectives. The enabling objectives directly aid the student in mastering the terminal objectives. *The relevancy objectives simply relate other content or skill areas to the terminal objectives for the very purpose of showing relevancy.*

Students are placed in a learning environment where the following is provided:

1. Students are given individual units of instruction within the course. These units are defined in behavioral objective terms. While a unit is difficult to define without the aid of an example, which will be given in the Design Format section following, a unit of instruction essentially means a *meaningful* unit of behavior, and is specified in the form of a behavioral objective. A unit is a task or concept of learning. Several units together make up what is commonly described as a course of instruction. The objectives referred to here will be called terminal objectives, and they make up the course for which we are primarily designing the instruction. These terminal objectives do not include objectives which are built around the primary or "core" course.

2. Students are also given specific "enabling" objectives to be achieved. They are labeled as "enabling" objectives in that the achievement of these objectives helps the student arrive at satisfactory performance of "terminal" objectives of the "core" course. The distinction between a terminal objective, and the "enabling" objective discussed here is as follows: Terminal objectives represent units of behavior such as done on the job or meaningful units of learning concepts for an academic course. Enabling objectives are background knowledge that must be mastered in order to eventually perform terminal behaviors. By way of a simple example, an enabling objective might be the identification of parts of a machine that must be mastered before the final terminal objective of operating a machine can be achieved. As will be elaborated upon in further detail below, it is the terminal objectives and enabling objectives together which make up

the central core of the Core Package, around which the remaining components are built to provide relevance to other areas of study.

3. Students are given behavioral objectives that relate directly to the terminal objectives of the core course, but which are not necessarily requirements for the achievement of such terminal objectives. These behavioral objectives are from designated content or skill areas outside the primary or core course that give additional relevance to the core course objectives. These are labeled as relevancy objectives. The terminal objective of operating a machine might have an objective from a science course on gears and levers. Such an objective is not necessary to perform the terminal objective of operating the machine, nor is it an enabling objective which is necessary as background knowledge that must be mastered to ultimately perform the terminal objective. Rather, it is an objective which shows the relevance between the core course and the study of science principles. The science principles might be from another course the student is studying, an area the student is just interested in, or an area to which, as teachers, we want the students to "see" a relationship. Objectives in the relevancy category could conceivably be several in number in relation to each terminal objective. This would depend on the number of other courses or discipline areas the designer or teacher wants to relate to the core course.

In summarizing, operationally the Core Package instructional design has three types of objectives, designed to meet three needs. These are:

1. Behavioral objectives to meet terminal (course) skill or content needs.
2. Behavioral objectives to assist the student in achieving the performance of terminal objectives,

called enabling objectives.

3. Behavioral objectives which relate to the terminal objectives, but only in the sense that they provide performance in skills or content areas other than what would be the primary purpose in taking the course. They are intended to show the relevance of other skills or content to terminal objectives being learned. Thus, they can be called relevance objectives.

It is the terminal and enabling objective of the three functional types of objectives which make up the "core" of the Core Package instructional design. The third type of objective meets the need of showing relevance—relevance of other skills or content to the core.

Specific operation of the Core Package calls for first giving the student a terminal objective, so that he will know what target of learning he is aiming to achieve. However, the student does not begin with the terminal objective and its associated learning, but rather with any enabling objectives which must be achieved first as background knowledge. Once the enabling objectives are achieved, he then has sufficient background to learn the terminal objective. And once the terminal objective is achieved, he can then proceed to objectives in the third category, the achievement of which will demonstrate relevance of other skills or content to the terminal objective. There may not be a requirement established in the operation of a Core Package course that students *must* learn the "relevance" objectives. These might be options, requirements, or a combination of both.

In the above description of the operational nature of the Core Package design, emphasis has been given to behavioral objectives, which play a functional role in instruction. They play the crucial role around which the design functions.

There are some other components of the design that help mediate the instruction towards these objectives. These other design components will be described under the Design Format.

Design Format

There are five components to a Core Package instructional design:

Purpose and Significance
Objective List
Terminal Objective Sheets
Enabling Objective Sheets
Relevance Objective Sheets

Purpose and Significance

As illustrated in Figure 6.1, the Purpose and Significance section is the opening statement of the total package. It explains why the course of instruction is of importance to students. It gives both an overview of what is to be learned, in goal-directed terms, and some affective qualities that the students will gain as a result of experiencing the course.

In job-oriented courses, a meaningful addition to the Purpose and Significance section is the inclusion of a job description. A job description serves not only to show students the relationship of their studies to an existing set of parameters about an eventual job, but for the designer the description becomes a beginning point to structure the course around specific behavioral objectives and content.

Objective List

As shown in Figure 6.2, the Objective List serves two purposes. First and foremost, it is a complete listing of all terminal objectives to be achieved, and thus provides an

Figure 6.1

PURPOSE AND SIGNIFICANCE

TELEVISION CAMERAMAN

Within the total system of television operations, the TV Cameraman plays a unique and special role. He is, in effect, the eyes of the audience. His camera is not simply a device to capture images before it, but rather his camera must be thought of as an extension of his own field of vision that will then become the field of vision for the audience that will immediately or ultimately view a live or taped program.

Under the direction of a Program Director, the TV Cameraman will use a video camera to photograph scenes for taping and broadcasting. This necessitates a great deal of knowledge and artistry on the part of the cameraman. He must know how to operate different types of video cameras and perform correct camera procedures, such as panning, tilting, dollying, and shot selection. Furthermore, his function in the total effort of television operations necessitates discussing dramatic and presentational effects, mood, and photographic composition of scenes with the Program Director. Knowledge related to basic physics principles, such as levers, is important because he must alter angles or distance of shots for effects.

As you progress through your course of study, it is important that you keep in mind the following goals:

1. Gain the necessary skills to effectively operate the video camera.
2. Appreciate the artistic necessity to produce a pleasing shot commensurate with the effect and mood desired.
3. Understand and cooperate within the total operation of television programming, including especially your role with other personnel.

See also: Dictionary of Occupational Titles, listing 143.062.

Figure 6.2

PERFORMANCE OBJECTIVE CHECKLIST

	DATE	DATE
NAME	ENTERED..........	COMPLETED..........

TELEVISION CAMERA OPERATION

When you have completed this course, you will: COMPLETION
                                                        DATE

1. Identify five major types of television cameras based on their use in the small studio, classroom, industrial training program, or large commercial studio.   ....

2. Describe the principles of photo-electricity, persistence of vision, and scanning as they relate to video camera operations. Sc. Sheet #1. Math Sh. #1.   ....

3. Describe four differences between a vidicon camera and an image orthicon camera. Assign. Sheet #1.   ....

4. Identify five different types of camera mounts. Assign. Sheet #2, 3, 4, 5. Sc. Sheet #2.   ....

5. Identify parts of a panning head and operate with smooth function. Assign. Sheet #6. Math Sh. #2.   ....

6. Identify and operate the major camera adjusting mechanisms of focusing control, panning tension control, lens turret control, tilting tension control, panning handle (guide arm), and handle angle adjustment. Sc. Sheet #3, Math Sheet #3, Assign. Sheet #7.   ....

7. Demonstrate proper focusing procedure on a static object. Assign. Sheet #8. Sc. Sheet #4.   ....

8. Operate the diaphragm opening (f-stop) of a video camera to demonstrate how the lens affects the depth of field. Assign. Sheet #13. Sc. Sheet #5, Math Sheet #4.   ....

9. Demonstrate proper focusing on subject moving toward and away from camera. Assign. Sh. #8. Sc. Sheet #6.   ....

10. Demonstrate simultaneous dollying and focusing. Assign. Sheet #9.   ....

(continued, next page)

overview in more specific terms as an extension of the Purpose and Significance. Second, it has an obvious administrative function, so that student and teacher can mark progress achieved. While these same objectives are to be found on individual Terminal Objective Sheets, a complete listing in one place will be of much value to student and teacher. Note in the illustration shown that the enabling and relevance objectives have been keyed to the terminal objectives to which they relate.

Terminal Objective Sheets

The terminology *normally* used for this component of the Core Package is not "terminal objective sheet." For the sake of illustration and to make the specific point that objectives used in this component are indeed "terminal" objectives, it has been convenient to refer to them as such. More often in practice they are called "Job Sheets," in the case of job-oriented training programs, or "Content Sheets," in the case of academic courses.

There are six parts to a Job or Content Sheet: (1) Objective, (2) Tools and Materials Needed, (3) General Instructions and Information, (4) References, (5) Procedures or Explanation, and (6) Questions.

The illustration shown in Figure 6.3 is from a job-oriented training program, and provides a convenient example to illustrate the various components and total applications of the Core Package. All one need do for more academic-oriented courses is to simply translate that part of the format called the Procedure, to Explanation. The Explanation would then involve a basic outlining of content towards the objective.

For each terminal objective listed in the Objective List, there is one job or content sheet. Each objective is dealt with separately, as a unit of instruction to be achieved by the

Figure 6.3

JOB SHEET 8

NAME .... APPROVED ....

1. OBJECTIVE:
   To be able to operate the diaphragm opening (f-stop) of a video camera to demonstrate how the lens affects the depth of field.

2. TOOLS AND MATERIALS NEEDED:
   A. Television studio camera
   B. 50mm. vidicon lens

3. GENERAL INSTRUCTIONS AND INFORMATION:
   For a specific lens, a large diaphragm opening (small f-stop number) will decrease the depth of field; a small diaphragm opening (high f-stop) will increase the depth of field.

4. REFERENCES:
   Assignment Sheet #13
   Television Production Handbook, Zettl, p. 29, 30
   Math Sheet #4
   Science Problem #5

5. PROCEDURES:
   A. Set up camera for studio production.
   B. Set 50mm. lens at f/1.9.
   C. Place three objects in front of camera; one 6 feet away, one 15 feet away, and the third 20 feet away.
   D. Note how many of the three objects are in focus.
   E. Focus on center object.
   F. Change f-stop to f/8 setting.
   G. Note number of objects still in focus and compare to results of f/1.9.
   H. Repeat procedures for f/22 setting.

6. QUESTIONS:
   Listed below are possible answers to the questions. Choose the correct answers and *WRITE* or *PRINT* them in the spaces provided.
                            increase   decrease
   A. If a 50mm. lens diaphragm setting is changed from f/1.9 to f/8, the depth of field will_____.
   B. If a 50mm. lens diaphragm setting is changed from f/22 to f/8, the depth of field will_____.
   C. If the diaphragm opening of a lens is increased, the depth of field will_____.
   D. See Instructor. Demonstrate objective.

ANSWERS:

A. Decrease
B. Increase
C. Decrease

student. It is around this objective that the remaining parts of the Job or Content Sheet are structured to help the student achieve the objective, and around which the remaining components (e.g., Assignment Sheet) of the Core Package are also structured.

The Tools and Materials, Part 2, are those physical items needed to perform the behavioral objective. In job-oriented programs, these are tools and materials. In academic courses, it might be such obvious things as a pen and paper, but might also include necessary materials in the way of charts or tools, such as a compass. The indicator for necessary tools and materials is the objective itself. Certain tools and materials will be required to do the performance according to the behavioral terms, and possibly others will be needed for stated conditions or standards of the objective. Note in Figure 6.3 that not all tools and materials are listed, but rather only those necessary outside of what could otherwise be easily implied.

Part 3, General Instructions and Information, can serve a variety of purposes. Essentially, it is intended to give some initial insight into the objective. In the illustration it is used to give some direct indication of what to expect. It could contain special points to watch out for, like dangerous areas of operation to be avoided. It could be a more specific descriptive explanation of the objective, with possibly a problem the student could answer to sample a part of the objective. Used in this way, the student could get some preliminary assessment of what he knows about the objective, or at least some idea of what is eventually in store. It could even include some affective descriptions of why it is important to achieve the objective, and what it is used for, or how it relates to other objectives. In general, then, this part can serve a variety of instructional and informational needs.

Part 4, References, is self-explanatory. While text

references most often make up what is specified, it could include films, tapes, and so forth. One essential thing to include, as shown in Figure 6.3, is the references to other components of the Core Package, such as an Assignment Sheet.

Part 5, the Procedures or Explanation, is specifically for instructional purposes. It outlines the procedure to be followed in learning the objective; or, in the case of an academic subject, it is the explanation of content concerning the objective.

There is nothing to stop the designer from including in the Procedure the questions that provide necessary inter-action. Note in Figure 6.3 that the questions have been placed in a separate section, Part 6. Wherever the questions may appear, in the Procedure or separately in Part 6, they must be provided, for interaction purposes. Immediately following the questions, direct feedback on the correctness of the responses should be provided, such as at the bottom of the Job Sheet.

Enabling Objective Sheets

In the operational description for the Core Package, it was stated that the student is given the Job Sheet first, so that he will be aware of what terminal performance is to be achieved. However, under most circumstances, the student does not immediately begin instruction by directly working with the Job Sheet. Usually, there are certain "enabling" objectives which must be achieved first so that the necessary background knowledge related to performing the terminal objective is known. For instance, using the illustration of learning the operation of the diaphragm opening, shown in Figure 6.3, it is doubtful that the student could perform this objective without first knowing the location of certain parts of the lens. Identification of the parts of a lens would then be an enabling objective, to be achieved prior to attempting the terminal objective.

Obviously, if a student can already perform an enabling objective (that is, it exists in his entry level performance capabilities), he need not work on this objective, any more than if he could already perform a terminal objective.

Possibly for lack of better terminology, an enabling objective sheet is most often referred to as an Assignment Sheet. An Assignment Sheet has one enabling objective related to a terminal objective of a Job Sheet. Obviously, there may be more than one Assignment Sheet for a given terminal objective; or, at the opposite end, no Assignment Sheet.

Figure 6.4 illustrates the design format for an Assignment Sheet related to the Job Sheet in Figure 6.3. There are four parts to an Assignment Sheet: (1) Objective, (2) General Instructions and Information, (3) References, and (4) Questions.

Part 1, the Objective, is the statement of the enabling objective to be achieved, related to a terminal objective in a Job Sheet.

Part 2 of the Assignment Sheet, the General Instructions and Information, serves the very same general use as it does for the Job Sheet. Any special instructions (e.g., use extreme care in handling the fragile lens) or information that gives more meaning to the objective can be included.

Part 3, the Reference, contains content sources that can be used to learn the enabling objective.

Part 4 of the Assignment Sheet, Questions, contains those necessary response items that will be used to practice and demonstrate satisfactory learning of the objective. Note in Figure 6.4 how the question directly measures the stated enabling objective. One thing to be noted about this particular objective is that it calls for identification of *some*

Figure 6.4

ASSIGNMENT SHEET 13

NAME .... APPROVED ....

I. OBJECTIVE:
    To be able to identify parts of a lens.

II. GENERAL INSTRUCTIONS AND INFORMATION:
    The function of a lens is mainly to produce a small, clear image of
    the viewed scene on the television picture tube. The lens you use
    determines how close or how far away an object will appear
    (assuming a fixed distance from camera to object). Some lenses
    make an object seem far away, although the camera is compara-
    tively close to it; other lenses show the object or action at close
    range, although the camera may be located at some distance from
    it.

III. REFERENCE:
    Television Production Handbook, Zettl. Job Sheet #8.

IV. QUESTION:
    Identify the following parts:

    ..... f-stop adjustment ring   ..... mounting threads
    ..... f-stops   ..... lens grip
    ..... distance (in feet)   ..... focus adjustment ring
    ..... optics   ..... mount

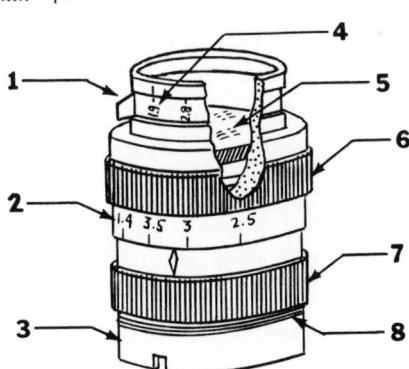

ANSWERS	
1	8
4	7
2	6
5	3

parts of the lens, the knowledge of which is not necessary in order to perform the terminal objective in the Job Sheet of Figure 6.3. In fact, this particular Assignment Sheet is used for more than one Job Sheet, as there are other terminal objectives in this course where identification of such items as the "mount" and "optics" is necessary. Thus, one Assignment Sheet may serve more than one Job Sheet, at times.

Relevance Objective Sheets

The discussion now changes from a consideration of the "core" components of the total Core Package to those components that are included in the "package" to show the relevance of other subjects to the core.

Relevance can be exhibited in many ways. What is used to show relevance, however, is not a haphazard selection of just anything. Selection should be judged against those things that would first have meaning to the student and then show relevance to the core course.

It is much easier to select subject areas of relevance when the student is engaged in many courses of study. A concurrent variety of courses also provides the opportunity to administratively strengthen the implementation of the Core Package as a whole, particularly in terms of the instructional aid that can be given to the student. For instance, suppose the core course is an economics course. Suppose further that students of this course were also engaged in concurrent courses in mathematics and political science. It is conceivable that certain terminal objectives learned in the economics course could be shown to have relevance to mathematics and political science.

Relevance Objective Sheets may be called many things. Figures 6.5 and 6.6 illustrate two situations that relate to the Job Sheet shown in Figure 6.3. Figure 6.5 illustrates a Math Sheet that shows how mathematics might be related to the

Figure 6.5

MATH SHEET 4

NAME .... APPROVED ....

I. OBJECTIVE:
    To be able to calculate problems using the Inverse Square Law as it
    applies to determining Relative Aperture Ratios (a factor used in
    calculating depth of field).

II. MATERIALS NEEDED:
    A. Pen and Paper.

III. GENERAL INSTRUCTIONS AND INFORMATION:
    Depth of Field is that area in which all things appear to be in focus. It is
    measured from the point nearest the camera which is acceptably sharp
    to the point farthest from the camera which is acceptably sharp. In the
    accurate calculation of Depth of Field, several mathematical concepts
    are brought to bear, including among others the "Inverse Square Law."
    This law, in turn, involves knowledge of basic concepts related to how
    numbers are squared and how ratios are expressed.

IV. REFERENCES:
    JDD, Chapter 7
    HFB, Chapter 4
    RM, Chapter 2

V. PROCEDURE (INSTRUCTION):
    A. Review the meaning of ratios (JDD, pp. 229-230).
    B. Review the procedure for squaring a number (RM, p. 48).
    C. State the mathematical relationship expressed in the Inverse Square
        Law (HFB, Chapter 4, p. 41).
    D. State the formula for calculating relative aperture ratio (f/number).
    E. State the relationship between the Inverse Square Law and the
        relative aperture ratio formula.
    F. State the effect on f/number when the diameter (D) of a lens
        decreases; increases. (HFB, p. 42).

VI. QUESTIONS:
    A. As the diameter of the lens opening (increases/decreases)
        _____, the f/number will be increased.
    B. If the focal length of a given lens is 8 in. and the diameter of the
        maximum effective aperture is 2 in., the relative aperture would
        be?_____
    C. If the focal length of a given lens is 4 in. and the diameter of the
        maximum effective aperture is 1 in., the relative aperture would
        be?_____
    D. If the focal length of a given lens is 2 in. and the diameter of the
        maximum effective aperture is 4 in., the relative aperture would
        be?_____

FOR ANSWERS, SEE
NEXT PAGE

Figure 6.6

SCIENCE PROBLEM 5

NAME .... APPROVED ....

I. OBJECTIVE:
Describe the position and characteristics of the images formed by a convex lens for different positions of an object; cite an application appropriate for each.

II. MATERIALS NEEDED:
A. Convex lens (of known focal length)   C. Meter stick
B. Light box with wire screen   D. Cardboard screen

III. GENERAL INSTRUCTIONS AND INFORMATION:
You are going to perform an experiment to demonstrate the relationship between the position of an object relative to the focal length of a convex lens and the size of the object as it is projected on the opposite side of the lens on a screen. The importance lies in the practical application to which such relationship is necessary for the lens in a TV camera. You are to set up the experiment as described in TC, page 199, and position the object (the light source) as specified in the left hand column of the table below. Record your observations in the remaining three columns. The references listed below will provide you sufficient background to set up and record your observations.

IV. REFERENCES:
Taffel, Visual Physics, pp. 199-205
UNESCO, p. 180
TC Workbook, pp. 199-200

V. PROCEDURE:
After reading the references listed above, position the object as described in the left hand column of the following table. Record your observations.

Position of Object	Position of Image	Description of Image	Applications
1. Infinitely far from lens			
2. At a distance from lens greater than twice the focal length (2F)			
3. At twice the focal length (2F)			
4. Between one and two focal lengths (F and 2F) from lens			
5. At the principal focus (F)			
6. Between the principal focus (F) and the lens			

FOR ANSWERS, SEE
NEXT PAGE

terminal objective of operating the diaphragm opening of a video camera. Figure 6.6, in like manner, illustrates how a science problem relates a physics principle to the same terminal objective. The basic intent in both instances is to show the student the relevance of other areas of study; or it could be an area of student interest.

As illustrations of Relevance Objective Sheets, note that the design format of both the Math Sheet and Science Problem is the same as the Job Sheet to which they relate. Furthermore, the statement of the objective not only relates a behavioral intent in the area of relevance, but also does another thing. Using the Math Sheet as an example, note that it is essentially a math-related objective; however, it also relates back to the original terminal objective, in this instance the content of "depth of field."

Those parts of the design format related to Tools and Materials, General Instruction and Information, and References are self-explanatory, serving the same basic purposes as in the Job Sheet, except that they are stated in terms of the Math Sheet objective. Many times the General Instructions and Information section remains the same for both Job Sheet and Relevance Objective Sheet, although specialized information or instructions can be written for each if required.

In terms of the Procedure part of the design format, two different approaches have commonly been used. One involves leaving the Procedure the same way, word for word, as it is in the Job Sheet. In this case, the intent is to let the reference do the sole job of providing content; and the Procedure is left as it is in the Job Sheet, so that the student can refer to it and see directly how the Math is related. The second way to use the Procedure part is for instructional purposes, as related to the objective of the Relevance Objective Sheet. In this instance, the Procedure part is as it appears in Figure 6.5. It is a procedure for math, rather than the procedure of the terminal objective on the Job Sheet. The use of the Procedure part for specific instruction is probably preferable, as the student can gain the same advantage attributed to using the Job Sheet's procedure by simply referring back to it.

Finally, the Questions part of the design format contains questions related to providing interaction with and practice towards the objective. Of course, such questions need not be put into a separate section as illustrated here. They could appear in the Procedure part at appropriate points of instruction.

Outcomes Expected

The usual outcomes associated with nearly any interactive instructional design can be associated with the Core Package. What distinguishes this design from others is that it is *a direct attempt at showing relevance between what the students are principally learning and other courses that they are taking and/or areas of special interest to students.* The outcome is not only to demonstrate relevance, but also to develop motivation. If students can see the relevance of what they are studying to areas of "real" interest to them, then their motivation to learn can certainly be expected to increase. This is not to say that what they are learning in a given course or training program is itself not of interest or relevance to students, but only that other areas of study can show relevance as well. If for some reason a given course does not seem to be relevant to the students, then other means must be sought to show relevance. In this sense, the Core Package approach will be significant.

Outside of demonstrating relevance for the student, one particular outcome related to program administration will be of interest to teachers. When the Core Package approach is used in an instructional setting in which the student is undertaking the study of several courses, teachers have the instructional basis upon which to work more closely with one another.

CHAPTER VII

TRI-LEVEL STUDY GUIDE

Use

It is doubtful that any instructional program can truly take into account and meet all the varying course entry level skills of students. As a matter of common practice, most programs or courses are designed on one level of instruction, and it is generally hoped that most students will succeed within the level. But there are ways around this "shotgun" approach to instruction. Since students do enter courses with varying degrees of knowledge about the objectives of a course in general and about specific objectives to be achieved, this variance should be accounted for and provisions made so as to improve learning efficiency and effectiveness.

Even in those instances when a course has been fully validated, the result has been to lower the level of instruction so that even the few students who know nothing about the content can achieve within that instruction. That is not necessarily bad, but what it does mean is that, for certain objectives, some, if in fact not many, students can already satisfactorily perform or at least need only a minimum of instruction to perform. The design discussed in this chapter is an attempt to account for and meet this problem of varying student entry levels.

The Tri-Level Study Guide is an attempt to account for student entry level knowledge at three levels: (1) students with complete knowledge about a given objective can test that knowledge to reaffirm it as truly being something they know; (2) students who enter with some, but not all, the knowledge about an objective can acquire whatever they lack in a short period of "informational" time and then test themselves; and (3) students who know nothing or very little about an objective can get complete instruction that brings them up to the level of satisfactory performance. The Tri-Level Study Guide design can be used by individual learners working within the classroom, or it can be used outside the classroom—as preparation for classroom group work.

The Tri-Level Study Guide does not presume to account and provide for *all* possible student entry levels relative to all objectives. But it does not presume that just one level of instruction should be given to all students. It does suggest that there is an efficient and effective way to mediate the instruction for those students who can already perform an objective or need only a minimum of information to successfully perform the objective. The latter group of students includes both those needing only certain reminders of content they previously knew but have forgotten, and those who need a minimum of new content knowledge which they lack to otherwise satisfactorily perform an objective. And, of course, there is the third level of instruction, of a more complete nature, to meet the needs of those students who know nothing, or very little, about the content needed to reach an objective.

Operational Description
The operational description which follows will show how this design provides instruction at three possible levels of student entry level knowledge. First, there is a description of what the three levels of instruction have in common,

followed by how each is provided for individually.

As discussed under the *Use* section, the Tri-Level Study Guide is an attempt to prescribe instruction for students at three levels of possible entry level knowledge. In the very strict sense, one would have to say that there are really only two levels of "instruction" in this design. This is because the first-level students, those who have the existing performance capability to demonstrate knowledge of a given objective and need only a means to reaffirm it, do not receive "instruction." Such students do not receive new information, interact with content, or receive confirming feedback to such information and interaction. They are provided criterion testing, which is a part of effective instruction. But, without worrying about semantics, consider the first level as involving instruction.

No matter what entry level a student is at when he enters the use of a Tri-Level Study Guide, he will use two parts of the instructional design in common with any other student. These are: (1) a behavioral objective, and (2) a criterion test item(s).

The first thing the student is given is a behavioral objective. It defines what he is to learn and how he is to demonstrate that he has learned. To demonstrate learning, a criterion test item is provided to adequately measure the objective. Some further description about this criterion item is necessary.

When feasible, the criterion test item should allow for testing in exactly the same manner as stated in the objective. For example, if "explain" is the behavioral specification of the objective, then "explain" should be used in the criterion test item. If, however, a simpler, more easily used, discrimination-type question (i.e., multiple-choice, true-false, etc.) would just as accurately measure the behaviors, then by all means use the simpler form of questioning.

Knowing that all students have objectives and criterion test items in common, operationally the three levels of instruction are provided in the following way:

1. Students who enter with an entry level knowledge equivalent to the objective to be achieved—that is, they have the existing capability to perform the objective without further instruction—simply read the objective, determine for themselves that they can demonstrate the performance specified in the objective, and *prove it* by completing the criterion test item(s). They are given the correct answer to the criterion test to check against. Students unable to perform at this level then drop to the second level of instruction.

2. The second level of instruction is for those students who enter with either (1) a fair degree of entry level knowledge about the objective, and need only a minimum of new knowledge, or (2) need only certain reminders of content related to the objective so that they can perform the objective. They have already read the objective and the criterion item, but have not answered it because they think they cannot demonstrate satisfactory performance. The student could have tried the criterion test item, but for reasons to be shortly elaborated upon, it is better if they do not try it unless they *really* think they can perform. In any case, such students proceed to a part of the Tri-Level Study Guide containing summary information and general instruction. This part of the design contains sufficient information to bring them up to a satisfactory level of performance, so that they can go back to the criterion test item and satisfactorily demonstrate performance. To summarize, a student at the second level (1) reads the objective, (2) reads the criterion test item, but does not answer it, (3) reads information and instructional content related to the objective which is presented on a gross, overview basis, and (4) then

answers the criterion test item, checking the answer to confirm his own performance. If a student is unable to perform on his level, he drops to the third level.

3. Students with little or no entry level knowledge relative to the objective proceed in the same manner as the students in Level Two above. After reading the general information and instructions, students in the third level have determined that even the gross, overview information is not sufficient for them to perform satisfactorily on the criterion test item. Having made this determination, they must proceed to more detailed instruction, which is contained in another section of the study guide. In this section they receive detailed reading, practice, and interaction with content. Finally, they culminate their activity by use of the criterion test item to prove that they have achieved the objective.

It is obvious in the above description that this design places a decision-making role *upon the student.* He must determine whether or not he thinks he is able to complete the criterion test item. A well-written objective will make this decision-making role easy for the student. While he may try the criterion test item at any time he wishes, there is the possible problem that, in attempting the criterion item two or three times and checking the answer, the student becomes attuned to the correct answer. More will be said about this in the Design Format.

In summarizing the operational description of the Tri-Level Study Guide, the three entry levels are provided for as illustrated in Figure 7.1. Level One students are those who enter with an existing performance capability of the objective, and use only the objective and criterion test item. Level Two students are those who enter with fairly high entry level knowledge, and use the objective, receive brief overview information, and use the criterion test item. Level Three

Figure 7.1

LEVEL	ENTRY LEVEL KNOWLEDGE
1	Complete knowledge of objective
2	High but not complete knowledge of objective, or needs only reminders of content
3	Low or no existing knowledge of objective

LEVEL	PARTS OF DESIGN USED
1	Objective. Criterion Test Item
2	Objective. General Information. Criterion Test Item
3	Objective. General Information Instruction. Criterion Test Item

students are those who enter with little or no entry level knowledge, and use the objective, general information, detailed instruction, and finally the criterion test item.

Design Format

There are five parts to the Tri-Level Study Guide, as follows:

Objective
Criterion Test
General Information
Instruction
Answers

Objective

It is generally the case, in using this design, that the objectives of the course are treated individually. As always, the purpose in stating an objective is to communicate to the student the specific behavioral outcome expected.

Figure 7.2 illustrates the Tri-Level Study Guide format. Note that the first part of the design with which the student is confronted is the behavioral objective. As stated in the Operational Description, the objective is one of two parts which all students use in common, no matter what their entry level knowledge might be.

Criterion Test

The second part of the instructional design, and the second item the students use in common, is the Criterion Test section. The illustration given here shows that this particular objective can be tested in either of two ways, not that both ways must be written into the study guide. In actual use, the teacher would normally want only one form of the question. The multiple-choice form would be the

Figure 7.2

STUDY GUIDE

OBJECTIVE: Given the lengths of two sides of a right triangle, calculate the length of the third side so as to demonstrate the Pythagorean Theorem.

Criterion Test:

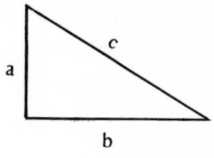

If side a is 6 in. and side b is 8 in. in the triangle at the right, what is the length of side c? (check p. 14 for answer)

(Depending on students, the following discrimination-type question might be a suitable substitute for the above:
Which of the following equations and/or problems correctly express the relationship between a, b, and c in the given triangle (of the illustration above)?

.....a. $a^2 + b^2 = c^2$ .....d. side c equals 10 in.
.....b. $b^2 + c^2 = a^2$ .....e. $6 + 8$ equals $\sqrt{14}$
.....c. $b = \sqrt{c^2 - a^2}$ .....f. $c = 14$

GENERAL INFORMATION

The Pythagorean Theorem is one of the most useful theorems in mathematics. It states an important relationship between the lengths of the legs and the length of the hypotenuse of a right triangle. The theorem states that in any right triangle the square of the hypotenuse is equal to the sum of the squares of the legs.

INSTRUCTION

Read pages 265-266 of JDD, then answer the following: (Answers—p. 14)

1. State the Pythagorean Theorem.
2. The Pythagorean Theorem applies to:
   .....a. all triangles   .....c. right triangles
   .....b. equilateral triangles   .....d. isosceles triangles
3. If the hypotenuse of a right triangle is expressed as c and the sides as a and b, how would the equation be expressed for the Pythagorean Theorem?
4. Calculate problems 1-5 on page 269 of JDD.
5. Calculate the Criterion Test Item above. (check page 14 for answers)

easiest to administer and use, although the other form is the more accurate indicator, as it is exactly the same behavior as specified in the objective. The essential point to be made is that the criterion test item is the second part of the Tri-Level Study Guide, and all students will use it, no matter what their entry level knowledge might be.

General Information

The purpose of this part is to present information which explains the content of the objective in gross, overview terms. The General Information section is really meant for information and not instruction, although in a sense it does provide instruction. As used here, the word instruction means the process of presenting content *and* the associated, built-in interaction so that the student can test his understanding of the content. Information is the presentation of content without interaction. Note in Figure 7.2 that the information is gross, overview content which would require the student to already know something about what is being presented. For example, if a student reading this information did not know what the hypotenuse was, he probably would not be able to understand what was being presented. What is written into the General Information section is information which assumes some entry level knowledge, and is intended to present general, overview content related to the objective.

Instruction

Part Four of the Tri-Level Study Guide format is the Instruction section. Here, detailed guidance is given to the specific resources and materials to be used or read. In addition, interaction is provided in the form of questions, the answers to which will eventually lead to satisfactory performance on the criterion test item. Figure 7.2 lists outside resource material for the detailed content. One could, of course, write the content into this section of the design, with the appropriate questions at points in the content where needed. Note in the illustration that questions 1, 2, and 3 are background questions which clarify certain aspects of the objective, while question 4 directs the student to further practice, if desired, and question 5 refers the student to the criterion test item.

Answers

Finally, Part Five of the Tri-Level Study Guide format is the Answers. These are answers to the criterion test item and the questions specified in the Instruction part. They are contained on a sheet separate from the other four parts of the design, and are not illustrated in this text.

Let us now turn to how these parts of the instructional design are used to meet the varying entry level knowledge of students.

Level One students, who have been described as those students with an existing performance capability on a particular objective, enter the Study Guide, as do all students, by reading the objective. They then read the criterion test item and determine, on the basis of having read both the objective and test item, that they can perform. They answer the criterion test item and check their results against the correct answer. If they have answered correctly, they then move on to the next objective.

Level Two students, those with a fairly high entry level knowledge but lacking certain knowledge, or those needing only reminders of content, proceed from the criterion test item, which they may or may not have tried, to the General Information section. They read this section and determine if they think they can now answer the criterion test item. They are, in effect, saying to themselves, "We have gained sufficient new information to enable us to answer the criterion test item." If they satisfactorily perform the objective by answering the criterion test item, they move on to the next objective. If not, they go to the Instruction part of the format.

Level Three students, those with little or no existing entry level knowledge relative to the objective, have by this time read the objective, the criterion test item, and the General Information. The General Information has given them an overview of the content, which they will now learn in detail by proceeding through the Instruction part. They use the Instruction part as directed, finally returning to the criterion test item to test their performance.

One final point should be made before closing the description of the design format. One problem confronting the designer of this study guide relates to the use of the criterion test item. In some instances, a student could possibly try the criterion test item and see the answer to that item twice. That is, the student might read the objective and try the criterion test item; and, failing to perform, then read the General Information and try the criterion item and still fail to perform. The question is, would this criterion test item still be able to serve its intended purpose, since the student in this instance has tried the question and seen the answer twice? He would know the answer without really having learned, so how can he test his performance capability? One possible solution is to write more than one form of the criterion test item. Figure 7.2 illustrates two forms of the criterion test item, one verbal and one based on discrimination. For certain types of objectives, another *example* can be written for the criterion test item rather than another form of the question. For instance, for the same objective in Figure 7.2, another problem with different values could be written for the calculation problem. The other form or example of the criterion test item would be placed after the

General Information, giving directions to the student to answer that criterion item rather than one he had already tried. If a third example is needed, it could be written at the end of the Instruction part. In this manner, the problem of a student using the same criterion test item throughout the study guide has been overcome. (Of course, some criterion test items, such as those requiring a demonstration of a skill, cannot be passed by "knowing the answer.")

While on the subject of the criterion test and how one could avoid or lessen the problem associated with the student becoming overly prompted to a correct answer, there is another possible design format for dealing with the problem. It does call for some restructuring of the format presented thus far, but only to a slight degree. It involves the use of a pre-test with the design. Figure 7.3 illustrates in flow-chart form how the design would operate, and indicates how the format would have to be restructured.

Essentially, the student would take a pre-test composed of criterion items designed to measure each objective of a particular lesson. In effect, rather than using each criterion test item separately, with its associated objective, as has been discussed as the format up to this point, the test items are grouped together in one test to be completed together. A student who is able to perform satisfactorily on questions in the pre-test would simply study only those objectives on which he failed to perform adequately. The questions which are incorrect would cue the student to the corresponding study guide sheet containing the objectives which he would read, followed by the General Information. He then tries another form of the criterion test item and, based on his performance, goes on either to another objective (as indicated by performance on the pre-test) or to detailed Instruction. After completing the Instruction part, he again attempts a criterion test item. In restructuring the format in

Figure 7.3

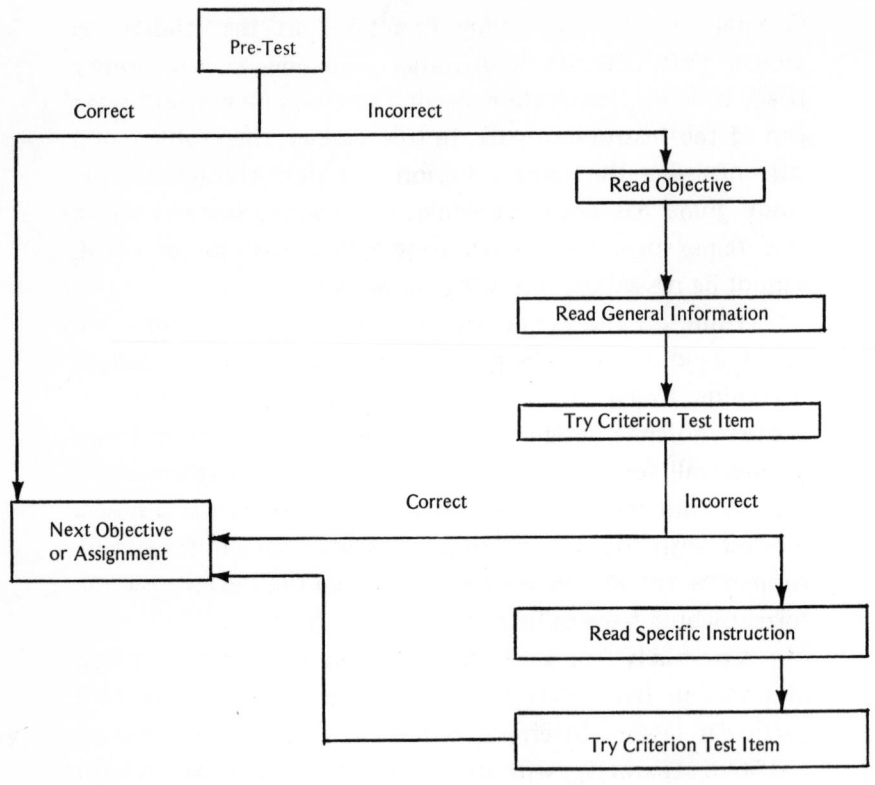

this manner, the pre-test simply removes the criterion test item one step away from the student's immediate instruction, and therefore lessens the possibility of his remembering the answer. If the pre-test were "scored" by a teacher, the answer would be totally removed. Restructuring the format in the above way, or staying with the format as originally discussed, is really a matter of how the designer wishes to administer the program. There are some points to be made in favor of either format.

Outcomes Expected

The principal outcome is the way the Tri-Level Study Guide facilitates learning for students. The Tri-Level Study Guide accounts for at least three possible levels of student entry level knowledge, and in that sense it provides for two more levels than most instructional designs. This is not to say that other instructional designs could not use the same basic framework of this approach, only that the usual course of instruction does not normally provide for it. In any case, from the standpoint of student use, they are provided the opportunity to apply any existing knowledge to what they are to learn, as specified by the learning objectives. Students will feel that instruction is being provided to *their own* instructional need-level.

Not only is there a student use benefit, but also a learning efficiency outcome that is a direct result of the way the student uses the instruction. Claim is often given to the idea that a course of instruction should be effective and *efficient*. Usually, only lip service is given to the efficiency factor. This instructional design deals directly with efficiency, in that it does account for varying entry levels. Because a student might only perform on what was described as level one, he can get through the instruction for some objectives in a minimum of time.

CHAPTER VIII

AUDIO-WORKBOOK

Use

With the current wide availability of cassette tape recorders, instructional designs involving the audio tape medium are no longer exotic and out of financial reach. One might believe that a recording studio and large associated expenses are still necessary to utilize audio, but such is really not the case. Instructional designs utilizing the audio medium have many uses that do not require or necessarily need the high degree of professionalism usually sought after. There are instances in which nonprofessional voice recordings, for instance, are best for communicating at a level which makes students feel more comfortable.

It was stated at the beginning of this volume that we would not discuss in detail procedures for producing instructional designs—that such procedures have already been covered in depth within other texts currently available for study. However, the lack of clear and substantive procedural guides given elsewhere to the development of the audio medium justifies the inclusion of a discussion of a procedure for the development of *this particular* instructional design. The procedural guide to audio program development will be included under the *Design Format* heading, and will be presented by an example of a project undertaken by the author.

Independent study via the use of audio tape cassettes is increasingly finding its way into training and education, both for at-home use and in "listening areas" within classrooms and libraries. However, this existing use of the audio medium is not itself the justification for use as an independent study means. Rather, it is the simple fact that the hardware most commonly used, the cassette player, is *designed for individual use.* Also, since the student may wish to replay, in the same sense that he re-reads a segment of a book, it makes sense to provide audio instruction for the individual to use as he would prefer. This is particularly crucial for individualized learning.

Allied to the topic of use is the topic of application. Application tells us when and in what manner to use audio, rather than simply its use based on independent study. Justifications for application fall into two categories.

The first application is for learning behaviors (objectives) that absolutely *need* an audio medium. For instance, if an objective called for the student to listen to a piece of music and identify certain notes or style, audio is required. Other objectives need audio to do the performance itself—for instance, in language training, or when the student is to role-play or give an oral presentation.

A second application which quite often justifies use of audio is that which relates to *facilitating* learning. This involves learning requirements in which the student must attend to more than one "slice" of information at a given time. For instance, when a student is reading detailed information relating to a chart, graph, or table, with various items physically separated from one another, he cannot both look at the chart and read the information. Typically, he finds himself reading a little, then holding his place in the book, and then glancing at the data-filled chart. You have been doing this in this book, when instructions have been given to look at an illustration. Worse yet, the problem is compounded by putting the chart on *another* page, which is often necessary. If, on the other hand, the student can *listen* to the information and look at the chart, he can attend to *both* functions. Therefore, when concurrent "attention" demands are placed on the student, particularly when detailed illustrative content is associated with reading, instruction is best taken care of by using audio.

Operational Description

The operational mechanics of an audio-workbook are simple, although varying levels of sophistication can be added in terms of developmental procedures that are followed, or in terms of the audio hardware itself. One is cautioned at this point not to let such sophistication prevent the use of this design.

The reason this design is called Audio-Workbook, rather than an audio design, is that the desirable characteristics associated with providing student interaction remain a basic requirement. As with any design, interaction is necessary for achieving higher levels of effectiveness and efficiency of learning. While a student could "record" his own interaction on audio tape, such mechanics of operation generally become more complicated than is normally required. Thus, the workbook is a more convenient means of interaction between the audio presentation and the student. Also, the workbook becomes, after its use, a much more convenient means for review purposes than an audio recording.

Operationally, the Audio-Workbook design functions as follows:

1. The student is directed to a set of written behavioral objectives. As with any design, these represent the learning targets to be achieved—in this case through listening and interacting with instructional content from the audio tape.

2. Having read the objectives, the student then listens to the audio tape. A presentation of content is given. As used here, content also includes illustrations that appear in the workbook (i.e., graphs, visuals, etc.).

3. At appropriate points in the presentation of content, directions are given to answer questions related to the objective being presented. Such questions are elicited in either of two ways. Directions can be given to answer a question printed in the workbook, or the question itself may be given on the tape, with the responses to be written in the workbook.

4. Confirmation of answers to questions are then given. Confirmations may either be printed in the workbook or given on the tape.

5. The student is then given directions to continue the audio presentation for additional content, questions, confirmation, or to proceed to a new objective.

Design Format

The design format has two components:

The Audio Tape
The Workbook

The Audio Tape

This particular component cannot be shown here and it would not be of any value if it were. However, it might be of some value to see the script from which the recording is made. The script will illustrate how you can set up your own script and what is required. As will be discussed later, *there may be no written script produced,* such as the one shown in Figure 8.1. If you do have a written script, note four things in particular. First, in paragraph 1, an overview approach is used to let the student know in general what is ahead of him.

Figure 8.1

Course 3
Assignment 13

SCRIPT

NARRATOR: This is the beginning of the review of assignment 6, entitled *"Premiums, Experience Rating, and Reserves."* This assignment is basically concerned with the cost of group life insurance. The first aspect dealt with is that of premiums. This is followed by a discussion of the net cost of group insurance, due to experience rating, and then by a discussion of acquired reserves. At the tone, stop the tape and turn to page 139 in your response booklet. (PAUSE.) Read the objectives on assignment 6, then restart the tape.

(TONE)

Rates for group life insurance must meet two objectives. First of all, they must be adequate. Secondly, they must be equitable. An *adequate rate* is one that provides, in the aggregate, enough premium income to meet the total expected losses, establish proper reserves, and pay for administrative expenses. An *equitable* rate means that a rate charged to a policyholder must reflect the value of the risk assumed for that particular policyholder plus his fair proportion of the expenses required. In other words, a particular policyholder that presents a risk which is higher than average should pay a premium that is higher than average. Now turn to page 140 in your response booklet and write your answer to question 1. (PAUSE.) You are to: "Describe the objectives of rate making as they apply to group life insurance."

(TONE)

Figure 8.2

Course 3
Assignment 13

When you have completed the Review of *Assignment 13*, you will:

1. State how an injured worker recovered damages from his employer under common law, and list the three common law defenses that the employer could use to defeat the worker's claim for damages.

2. Explain the fundamental principle of workmen's compensation in terms of employer liability and legal interpretation.

3. List the five fundamental objectives of workmen's compensation.

4. List the five major requirements that an injured worker must fulfill to collect workmen's compensation benefits.

5. Describe the four major types of workmen's compensation benefits that are available to injured workers.

6. Given a list of possible statements regarding the effectiveness of workmen's compensation, identify any correct statements.

Turn on the tape.

Second, again in the first paragraph, directions are given to read the behavioral objective printed in the workbook. Third, an indication is made of where a tone should be given as a signal for the student to stop the tape, when necessary. Fourth, directions are given to answer questions on specific pages. In the illustration, question 1 is asked on the tape. The direction could have been to a specific page where the question would be printed.

The Workbook

There are three parts to the workbook.

First, as shown in Figure 8.2, there is a page listing the behavioral objectives. Directions are given on the tape to read the objectives before listening to the content. A simple statement to "Turn on the Tape" is printed on the bottom of the page, telling the student to begin the audio presentation again.

Figure 8.3 illustrates a question page. Lengthy questions should be printed in the workbook. In the case of multiple-choice questions, this is always the case. Note that, in this particular illustration, directions are given at the bottom of the page as to where the confirmation is to be found. The confirmation appears on the page opposite (see Figure 8.5). If the confirmation is to be given on the tape, the following statement should be substituted: "The Answer is given on the tape. Turn on the Tape." Figure 8.4 illustrates another type of question page. In this instance, the question is given on the tape, and a blank space is provided for the student to write his answer. Note at the bottom of the page the directions to turn on the tape, as the answer in this case is given on the tape, although the directions (as in Figure 8.3) could have been to check the answer on a printed page opposite the question.

The third part of the workbook is the confirming

Figure 8.3

Course 3

Assignment 13

Question 5

Describe the major types of workmen's compensation benefits that are available to injured workers.

Check your answer on page 149.

Figure 8.4

Course 3

Assignment 13

Question 3

(When you hear the tone, write your answer below.)

The Answer Is Given on the Tape.
Turn on the Tape.

Figure 8.5

ANSWER TO QUESTION 5

Four major types of benefits are available:

1. The costs of hospital care, physician care, surgical and medical services are normally paid in full in most jurisdictions.

2. Disability income benefits are paid for stated periods depending on the degree of disability. Disability can be temporary total, permanent total, temporary partial, and permanent partial. The amount paid for disability benefits depends on the degree of disability.

3. Death benefits to the dependent survivors may be paid. These benefits include cash payments for stated periods and a funeral allowance.

4. Rehabilitation services are often provided to the injured worker.

Turn on the tape.

answer page. Figure 8.5 is a typical illustration. Of course, there is not always an answer page, as the answer could be given on the tape. When there is an answer page, directions should be given at the bottom to "Turn on the Tape," as shown at the bottom of this illustration.

There is one other form of direction to be given to the student, and that is when the presentation is finished, i.e., "This is the end of Lesson 1." Such a direction can be given on the tape or on the last page of a lesson, when the confirming answer to the last question is printed in the workbook. While this may sound like an obvious point, when you have an audio tape running, it is nice to know when you are indeed finished.

Finally, the workbook itself is not restricted to objectives, questions, and answers. Charts or simple visuals may be included as well. Thus, the simplicity of the Audio-Workbook instructional design can now be seen. Simplicity of design is one thing, but how you produce it is crucial—and somewhat more complicated.

Design Procedure

Written materials have always been produced (developed), quite naturally, from the written word. Audio as well has been traditionally produced *first* in the written word by means of the development of a script. The script is *written, then recorded.* Visuals have also traditionally been produced first in written form, as they are usually accompanied by either a written or audio description. The script is written and *then* visuals are added to accompany it. However, it would seem more logical to produce each medium "on its own terms."

When the desired message is to be *written,* production should be initiated in the written word only. Thus, a manuscript is written. If our intent is the production of an audio tape, it should *not* be produced initially in the written word. We should not write a script first. Rather, the intended *audio* medium should be produced in an *audio* format. This would be producing the medium on its own terms.

Since we are concerned with both a written medium (the workbook) and an audio medium (the audio tape) in this particular instructional design, the concept of producing a medium on its own terms can best be illustrated by means of an actual program production in which this was done. This program, entitled "The Cassette/Review Program," was developed at the Zimmerman Adult Learning Laboratory of the American College of Life Underwriters in Pennsylvania.

The Cassette/Review Program is made up of audio cassettes and accompanying workbooks—an Audio-Workbook instructional design.

The developmental procedure of the Cassette/Review Program involved ten basic steps. These steps are diagrammed in Figure 8.6. This description will provide a developmental procedure that you may use to develop your own Audio-Workbook instructional design. As a cautionary note, your attention is directed to the *basic procedure and concept,* not the people and facilities.

In *Step 1,* subject matter experts (in the content of the courses) were selected and brought together to attend an orientation session. This session involved an outline of the intent of the Cassette/Review Programs, how they would be produced, and the allocation of specific areas of responsibility for each subject matter person. A developmental control document was given to each subject matter expert, outlining the production steps, as shown in Figure 8.6

Step 2. The subject matter group was divided into teams of two for each course, and the group was supervised by an experienced program writer. Each subject matter expert was responsible for the development of seven or eight assignments of a fifteen-assignment course.

Step 3. This step involved the specification of the behavioral outcomes. One modification was made in our usual approach. Rather than having the subject matter expert delineate these outcomes as behavioral objectives, which would have involved extensive training of the subject matter expert in the technique of writing objectives, it was determined that the most effective existing skill of the subject matter expert was in the area of specifying questions and answers. Thus, for each assignment, the subject matter expert wrote a series of questions, with accompanying answers, as the specification of the outcomes expected of students in reviewing a given assignment. With the assistance of a programmer, each subject matter expert wrote the questions and answers which became the essential components of the workbook.

As *Step 4,* the questions and answers were turned over

Figure 8.6

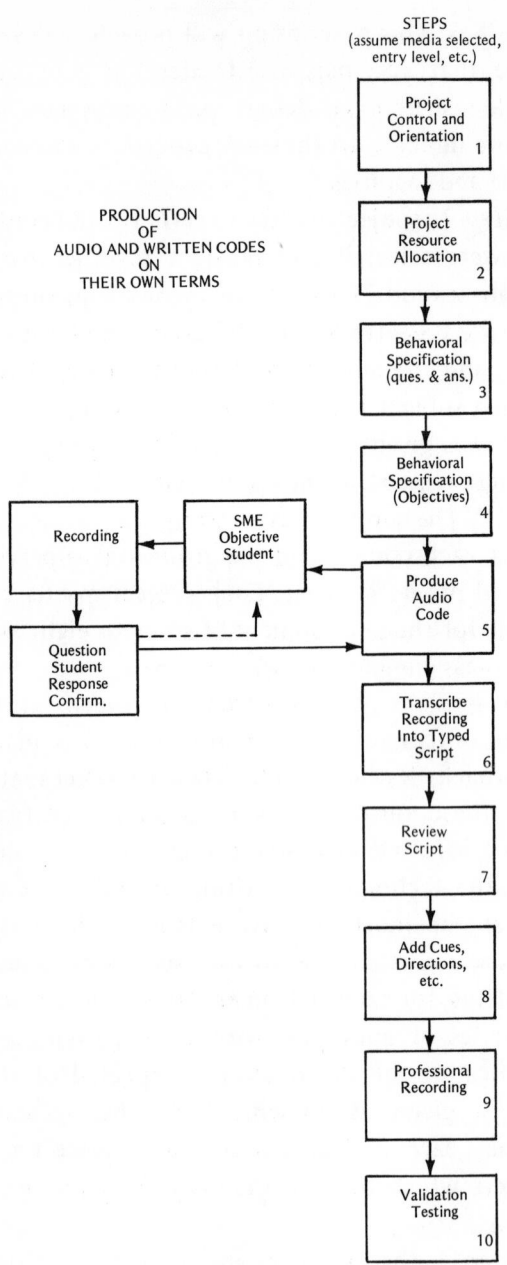

PRODUCTION
OF
AUDIO AND WRITTEN CODES
ON
THEIR OWN TERMS

STEPS
(assume media selected,
entry level, etc.)

Project
Control and
Orientation
1

Project
Resource
Allocation
2

Behavioral
Specification
(ques. & ans.)
3

Behavioral
Specification
(Objectives)
4

Recording

SME
Objective
Student

Produce
Audio
Code
5

Question
Student
Response
Confirm.

Transcribe
Recording
Into Typed
Script
6

Review
Script
7

Add Cues,
Directions,
etc.
8

Professional
Recording
9

Validation
Testing
10

to a programmer. The programmer, with experience in the specification of behavioral objectives, wrote objectives to match each of the questions. These objectives were then approved by the subject matter expert.

Step 5 involved the production of the audio component of the Cassette/Review Program. It was mentioned previously that traditionally this would have taken the form of the development of a *written* script. However, the concept of producing audio on its own terms was applied.

The subject matter expert sat down with a student and handed the student the objectives for a given assignment, which the student was then given time to read. He then turned on the tape recorder and *verbally* provided a review for each objective. It is important to note that he did not provide the review from a written script, but rather verbally produced a review. To establish a point of reference for the subject matter expert in producing such a review, he was told to view an objective as if it were a question being asked by a student. The subject matter expert was then to provide a verbal review of that objective.

At the end of his review for each objective, the subject matter expert gave the student the prepared question, to which the student wrote his answer. After completing the question, the student was given the confirming answer. After this, the student could give any feedback to the subject matter expert based upon the clarity of his verbal review.

When the subject matter expert had completed the recording of a review for each objective, he mailed the recordings to the Adult Learning Laboratory.

As *Step 6*, the recording was transcribed into a typed script. A word of caution should be noted here in the transcription process. That is, the wording is typed exactly as recorded. As a *simple* example, a word such as "it's" is not transcribed as "it is," since the former is the true component of the audio medium.

The essential point in Steps 5 and 6 is that the audio medium was initially produced on *its* own terms, that is, in audio. Production was initiated in audio, not the written code, for the development of an audio program. (Due to time constraints, in this project the production of audio on its own terms was not realized to the fullest extent possible. Instead of having the recording transcribed into a typed script in Step 6, the audio program from Step 5 could have been tested on a larger sample of students; then revisions made by further recordings [rather than on a written script basis]; and retested until the audio code was utilized to its fullest terms.)

Once transcribed, *Step 7* involved the subject matter expert's review of his audio recording, this time as a basic, first-draft, written script. He was cautioned to avoid changes that might in any way destroy the free flow and natural style of information that he had produced on the verbal level. Once he had reviewed the script, the script was then handed back to a programmer.

The programmer then reviewed the script as *Step 8*, adding appropriate cues, pauses, and directions to answering the questions that are a part of the workbook.

As *Step 9*, the script was then finished, with the approval of the subject matter expert and programmer, and professionally recorded.

Finally, as *Step 10*, developmental validation testing was then undertaken.

You might have reacted to this discussion of procedure, "But I don't have subject matter experts (I am the expert), programmers, typists, and professional narrators!" All those people, while helpful, are not necessarily required. If you have the facilities, you use them. If you are the subject matter expert, producer, writer, and teacher—all rolled into one—then utilize the procedure to the level of sophistication you can. Write your objectives, questions, and answers (the workbook) first. That is your target of learning and interaction. Get a student to sit down with you. Turn on the recorder and address yourself verbally to the objectives contained in the workbook.

Outcomes Expected

Active student involvement, through interaction provided by use of the workbook, should produce confidence in the student that he is learning. He is given the opportunity to test his understanding, and is given confirmation of the correctness of his responses.

Another outcome to be expected, because the Audio-Workbook is more than just an audio presentation, in that it requires active responding, is that student attention to content presentation will be higher. The student is not just a listener, but a performer as well.

Finally, when the Audio-Workbook is used to meet learning needs that demand "concurrent" student attention to details (i.e., discerning information from a detailed graph or table, while also listening to information that interprets the graph or table), we can expect additional learning effectiveness and much more learning efficiency (savings in learning time).

CHAPTER IX

INTERACTIVE TEXT

Use

A book on instructional designs would not be complete without a design that is addressed to the format of a self-contained text. "Self-contained text" is used here in the usual sense of meaning a written book or booklet containing all of the content in a subject matter area.

The textbook is the most widely used form of instruction. It is commonly used as a means of preparatory instruction prior to entering a classroom or as independent instruction that might culminate in a final examination. The term "text" has such a broad meaning in its general use that it should be defined in terms of how it is being used here, because the definition relates to its uses.

As defined here, the Interactive Text is used for *instruction* rather than *information*. On the surface it might seem artificial to draw a distinction between information and instruction; but, in terms of developing learning materials, it is useful to do so. When we know the purpose (*instruction* or *information*) for which the text is being written, then developmental efforts can be addressed more closely to the question of learning effectiveness. Knowing the purpose also relates to efficiency, both in terms of user time and in time and cost of development. Instruction is normally used when the intent is to initiate a change in behavior. Information is used to *inform* someone of facts and concepts. The distinction between information and instruction is more definitive when we consider how to approach the design of each.

When instruction is the text's purpose, then interaction is necessary so that the user (student) ultimately *knows* that he has learned. This means providing active responding, confirmation, and feedback. In the case of information, it is less critical that these be provided. For instance, the purpose of *this* book is primarily one of information—that you become familiar with different instructional designs. Obviously, this book also has the purpose of instruction, but it has not been the main purpose. No interaction has been provided. If this book were intended to be used in conjunction with a classroom situation, wherein you would be tested, then this book would have been written in the form of instruction, with active responding and feedback. Also, had such interaction and feedback been provided, then the amount of time it would have taken to develop and validate this book (an efficiency factor) and use it (also an efficiency factor) would have been increased. The effectiveness of this book also would have been increased, as it could have been tested by objective validation means. However, the purpose of this book is *information,* and thus interaction and feedback were not provided. While the book still achieves some change in cognitive behaviors (at least the author certainly *hopes* it has), the primary intent has been to produce in the reader *some familiarity* with different instructional designs that could be of use, without mandating a level of proficiency.

While the distinction between information and instruction is not always clear-cut, the manner in which it has been distinguished is useful in suggesting how to approach the presentation of content, particularly in the case of instruction. We generally know for what purpose we are writing a text, and that is for instruction. The problem is that, while we generally recognize the purpose, this is often not acted upon. If the purpose is to change behavior, then we use instruction, with its associated active responding, confirmation, and feedback. If the purpose is to remind someone of content or to change some behavior that is less definable, then we use an information approach.

In conclusion, the use of an Interactive Text is for an instructional purpose—*where a change of behavior is intended.*

Operational Description

Operationally, the student uses the Interactive Text in the following manner:

1. As an optional component, the student first enters the text by completing a pre-test. This test contains test items that measure each objective of the lesson or assignment about to be read. The student completes the pre-test, checks for correct answers, and enters the text at those points covering objectives for which he needs instruction. Specific reference is given by page numbers regarding where to enter the text for such objectives.

2. The student is given a set of behavioral objectives for the lesson or assignment. These are normally together in the front of the lesson, but they also can be placed at appropriate points within the text.

3. The student reads content directed towards each objective, with appropriate visual and graphic illustrations, as required.

4. During the presentation of content, appropriate background questions are asked, which are designed to clarify certain aspects of the objective. Confirmations to such questions are provided immediately after the questions.

5. At the end of content instruction, a question(s) is

asked which demands criterion performance as specified in the objective. This affords the student the opportunity to practice and test his having learned the objective. Confirmation is provided immediately after the criterion question.

6. Upon completing each individual assignment or chapter of a text, a post-test is completed by the student to determine which, if any, objectives have not been learned *as a result* of using the text. It tests each objective as did the pre-test, *and may in fact be the same test as the pre-test.* Specific reference is given to each test item, so that a student may go back into the text to review objectives on which he failed to perform as indicated by the post-test.

This operational description is not complicated. However, the Interactive Text is not like the usual type of text. It is more than information, in that its purpose is definitely instructional in nature. In addition to the fact that it contains behavioral objectives, its most distinguishing feature is that it is *interactive.* Interaction is provided within the body of the content materials, so that the student can assess his learning progress. He is provided confirming feedback to reinforce learning and to judge the correctness of his learning progress. As optional components of the text, pre- and post-tests can be added for purposes of providing the means for a student to "wash in" to the text to study only those objectives on which he needs instruction and to "wash back" into the text for additional study on those objectives not yet achieved. The post-test is also a means for the student to practice his retention of learning. When the design format is presented, it will be seen how other sources of content might be specified as an added aid to the student in clarifying content not otherwise learned in the text itself.

Design Format

There are six parts to an Interactive Text, the first and

last of which may be optional components. These are:

Pre-Test
Objectives
Content
Background Questions
Criterion Questions
Post-Test

Pre-Test

· The pre-test is a test designed to measure every objective of the text. It is composed of those test items necessary to measure the objectives of a given chapter or unit of instruction. For chapters covering many objectives, it is conceivable that the test could be further subdivided into two portions, so that one part covers the first half of the chapter and the second part the remaining half. There is nothing which says the pre-test must cover a complete chapter in one test situation—only that all objectives must be tested. And, of course, the test items must accurately and completely test each objective.

The purpose of the pre-test is twofold. First, it gives the student some assessment of what he does and does not know regarding the objectives to be studied. In the same sense, it also lets him know what is ahead of him in the way of content. Second, it has the purpose of showing what parts of the unit of instruction he can bypass and those which he must study. For this purpose, it is essential that the test items be valid indicators of the objectives.

Normally, the test items are sequenced in accordance with the same instructional sequence within the text itself, although there is some variation possible. In order to give the student direction into the text, so that he can bypass instruction not needed, specific references must be given with the test items as to where he should go within the text. This is accomplished by page references, such as illustrated by the pre-test shown in Figure 9.1. The page references are given with the answers to the pre-test.

The final thing to keep in mind about the pre-test is that it is not an absolute requirement for the Interactive Text. The function it can serve by being included is obvious. Through validation means, it might very well be determined that the pre-test is not needed—that the objectives contained in the text are not already part of student entry level knowledge and are therefore needed by all, or nearly all, students.

Objectives

The first absolutely necessary component of an Interactive Text is a set of behavioral objectives which outline expected learning outcomes. Objectives can be physically arranged in two ways. The first arrangement is a *list* of objectives at the beginning of a chapter. However, it is probably better that the objectives do not appear as just a list. It is suggested that a descriptive form be used, as illustrated in Figure 9.2. There is something about a descriptive form of stating the objectives that gets students to read the objectives—something not usually achieved by a listing of objectives. When a student sees a list, he is more apt to "scan" the list without careful reading, while the descriptive form will be more easily read.

The second way to physically arrange the objectives is to place the objectives within the body of text; for instance, after a content heading. This places the objectives more directly with the content that will describe them. It also provides what appear to the student as smaller increments of learning.

Figure 9.1

CHAPTER I PRE-TEST

You should be able to work each of the following problems on your computer. If you are unable to work any given problems, or you do a problem incorrectly, check the page reference given with the correct answer and proceed directly to that part of Section I dealing with the problem in question. Page numbers are given next to the answers to tell you where in the program to go for detailed instruction. Work all problems before checking answers.

1. Using your computer, divide 420 by 35. Answer..........

2. Using your computer, multiply 85 times 36.5. Answer..........

3. At what speed would you be flying to have covered a distance of 200 miles in two hours and thirty minutes? Answer..........

4. What would be the fuel consumption rate for an aircraft that in 1:30 used twenty gallons of fuel? Answer..........

5. What would be the True Airspeed of an aircraft showing an Indicated Airspeed of 140 mph, at a Pressure Altitude of 18,000 feet and a temperature of -20°C? Answer..........

6. What would be the True Altitude of an aircraft showing an Indicated Altitude of 24,200 feet, at a Pressure Altitude of 22,000 feet and a temperature of -10°C? Answer..........

ANSWERS	IF MISSED, PROCEED TO PAGE:
1. 12	p. 4
2. 3102.5 (approx. 3100)	p. 6
3. 80 mph	p. 8
4. 13.3 GPH	p. 12
5. 185.9 mph	p. 16
6. 26.000 feet	p. 20

Figure 9.2

CHAPTER I

INTRODUCTION AND OBJECTIVES

This text has been divided into three chapters for the purpose (1) of providing a logical breakdown of related problems; (2) to provide a block of calculations to be learned in one sitting; (3) to learn problems in the same order in which you will most likely use them during training.

It is suggested that you learn all the problems within a chapter in one sitting, then take a break before going to the next chapter.

Chapter I introduces you to the basic layout of an E6-B Flight Computer and to the very essential computations for both preflight planning and inflight calculations. You begin with a basic introduction by identifying the five basic parts of a flight computer. This is followed by direct application of these parts of a flight computer in the calculation of two preflight planning problems. The first type of problem involves giving you two of the three values for Time, Distance, and Speed, and you are to calculate the third, unknown value. The second problem involves giving you two of the three values for Fuel Consumption, Gallons Used, and Time, and you are to calculate the value of the third, unknown value. You will again note that both of these are preflight-type calculations, although there are occasions when they are also made during flight.

Finally, two basic inflight calculations will be learned—True Airspeed and True Altitude. To calculate the True Airspeed, you will be given the values of Pressure Altitude, Temperature, and Indicated Airspeed to then calculate the True Airspeed. True Altitude calculations involve some of the same given values as in calculating T.A.S. You will be given Pressure Altitude, Temperature, and Indicated Altitude to calculate the True Altitude.

Now turn to the next page to begin Chapter I.

Content

The third component of the Interactive Text is the content. What can be said about content? It should be clear and relevant to the objective being discussed. These are obvious requirements. But there is one thing about writing content that seems to escape most writers. That is, writers have *a tendency to keep secrets* when writing the content. They keep back content as if they might tell the student something that would give everything away. The philosophy should be to let everything be said that needs saying. Tell the student what it takes to achieve the objective he is trying to master. There are really few courses of study in which the content should be held back for the purpose of challenging the student to "think" and "analyze" for himself. Even in these courses, the "thinking" and "analysis" we want to promote are probably more a function of the concepts and principles themselves than the content. If you want to hold back content, wait until the student has first had a chance to learn. In other words, if content is to be held back, wait until practice exercises are given.

Criterion Questions

The six parts of an Interactive Text are listed above in the sequential order in which they would appear in the text. However, in order to describe the fourth part, the Background Questions, it will be necessary to describe next the fifth part, called the Criterion Questions. This is because background questions are determined in relation to the criterion questions.

The criterion questions are those questions which demand the same and complete performance as specified in the objectives. Note in Figure 9.3b that the question at the top of the page is a question that expects performance just as it is specified in the objective, which you see at the top of the

Figure 9.3a

FUEL CONSUMPTION

Objective— Given any two of three values for Fuel Consumption, Gallons Used, or Time, calculate the value of the third (e.g., given gallons used and time, find fuel consumption).

This type of problem is a proportion, represented by the formula:

$$\text{Gallons per hour (fuel consumption)} = \frac{\text{Gallons Used}}{\text{Time}}$$

There is no need to memorize this formula as it can easily be remembered by knowing the expression Gallons Per Hour (GPH) and what it means:

Gallons   is an expression of (fuel) gallons used

Per   is an expression the same as the sign — in a fraction

Hour   is an expression of time

$$\frac{\text{Gallons Used}}{\text{Time}}$$

Gallons Per Hour is an expression of two values, which are .... and ....

Answer
Gallons Used
and Time

Fuel consumption problems are worked exactly the same as Time-Distance-Speed problems. Both are proportion-type problems. Since fuel consumption problems involve an expression of time in hours, you will again have to remember to use 60 on the movable scale as your index under GPH in the proportion. The proportion, from the formula, looks as follows:

$$\frac{\text{GPH}}{60} = \frac{\text{Gallons Used}}{\text{Time}}$$

Which two values in the proportion above would appear on the movable scale when the problem is set up on the computer? .... and ....

Answer
60 & Time

Look at Figure 7. (Not shown in this illustration.) Suppose that thus far in your flight you have used 40 gallons of fuel and have been flying for a period of 3:30. What would your fuel consumption be? As a proportion, the problem would look like this:

$$\frac{\text{GPH}}{60} = \frac{40}{3:30}$$

Here you simply move the time, 3:30 on the inner (movable) scale, under the gallons used, 40 on the stationary scale, and then find the answer to GPH by reading it on the stationary scale above the 60 on the movable scale. What is the GPH? ....

Answer
II.4 GPH

Figure 9.3b

It should be obvious in fuel consumption problems that you could be given the fuel consumption (GPH) and some other value, such as Time, and be asked to find the gallons used. Given a fuel consumption of 15.8 GPM over a flying time of 1:50, how many gallons of fuel would have been used? Work as a proportion and write your answer here:............

Answer
20 Gallons

Here are some additional problems to practice on:

	Fuel Consumption	*Time*	*Gallons Used*
(1)	12.65 GPH	1:30	....
(2)	....	2:40	34.2 gallons
(3)	11.1 GPH	2:20	....

ANSWERS

(1) 19 gal.   (2) 12.8 GPH   (3) 25.9 gal.

page in Figure 9.3a. This criterion question measures the objective. It is then followed by three practice problems that also test the objective, and which might therefore also be called criterion questions.

There is nothing overly difficult about writing criterion questions. Just remember that the question must test the objective as it is stated. The question should not test just part of the objective or test the objective in some manner other than the behavior specified. You are simply providing the means for the student to test for himself whether he has achieved the objective in the manner specified by the objective. You can follow the criterion questions with other practice questions when possible, and if needed.

The purpose of providing questions in an Interactive Text is twofold. One is to provide the student with the opportunity to test if he has learned. The second relates to the idea that the student should not be just an idle reader. He should interact. Such interaction is particularly crucial when the student answers criterion questions, for he is being given the means to test for himself whether he has achieved an objective. Interaction via questioning is also important for the student in checking to see if the content related to an objective has been learned correctly up to that point where the criterion performance itself is demanded. That is, the student should interact with the bits and pieces of content that finally culminate in answering the criterion question.

Background Questions

The "intermediate" interaction suggested above is labeled as background questioning. Background questions simply test certain aspects of the content that describe the objective. Yet it is not simply a random form of questioning. Background questions are determined by a careful analysis of what it is about the objective that needs clarification in bits and pieces, and how those bits and pieces can be tied together. You can determine background questions by answering some of the following:

1. What *conditions*, implied or stated, in the objective need clarification?
2. What *standards*, implied or stated, in the objective need clarification?
3. What special terms need defining?
4. What terms (words or concepts) must the student discriminate (show differences or similarities) between?

Referring to Figure 9.3a again, all the questions seen on this page are background questions. They clarify certain aspects of the objective and eventually they are all put back together, so that the student then answers the criterion question at the top of Figure 9.3b.

Post-Test

Finally, the sixth part of an Interactive Text is the optional post-test. Actually, the post-test should be considered less of an option than the pre-test, as lack of satisfactory performance on any objective here would indicate that added instruction or review is necessary.

The post-test, as illustrated in Figure 9.4, can be exactly the same test as the pre-test for a given chapter, or, for objectives that can be tested by other examples, it could be a different test. However, it must test all the objectives and test them in the manner specified by the objectives.

One additional feature of the post-test that was not included when discussing the pre-test, in terms of specific page references, is that additional references to other texts and instructional materials can be added. That is, not only is

Figure 9.4

CHAPTER I POST-TEST

You should be able to work each of the following problems on your computer. If you are unable to work any given problem, or you do a problem incorrectly, go back and review that part of Chapter I dealing with the problem in question. Page numbers are given next to the answers to tell you where in the program to go for review, or you may wish to use one of the other references listed. Work all problems before checking answers.

1. Using your computer, divide 420 by 35.   Answer..........

2. Using your computer, multiply 85 times 36.5.   Answer..........

3. At what speed would you be flying to have covered a distance of 200 miles in two hours and thirty minutes?   Answer..........

4. What would be the fuel consumption rate for an aircraft that in 1:30 used twenty gallons of fuel?   Answer..........

5. What would be the True Airspeed of an aircraft showing an Indicated Airspeed of 140 mph, at a Pressure Altitude of 18,000 feet and a temperature of -20°C?   Answer..........

6. What would be the True Altitude of an aircraft showing an Indicated Altitude of 24,200 feet, at a Pressure Altitude of 22,000 feet and a temperature of -10°C?   Answer..........

ANSWERS	*IF MISSED*	
	REVIEW PAGE	*OR READ*
1. 12	p. 4	MR p. 10
2. 3102.5 (approx. 3100)	p. 6	MR p. 12
3. 80 mph	p. 8	MR pp. 4-5
4. 13.3 GPH	p. 12	HFR p. 48
5. 185.9 Mph	p. 16	HFR pp. 49-50
6. 26,000 feet	p. 20	MR pp. 13-15

an indication given to the student as to where he can go back into the text to review content for objectives not mastered, but other resources can be indicated which also cover such objectives. In this way, the student might find these other resources of value in learning the objectives he did not master—which apparently he was unable to master from the instruction received in the text itself.

In summary, the Interactive Text is composed of the following: A pre-test assesses student entry level knowledge. This can allow the student to by-pass what he already knows and to enter the text to learn only what he does not know in the way of objectives. Each area of content is introduced by objectives which tell the student what he is to learn and in what manner he is to demonstrate his learning. Appropriate and sufficient content is presented relative to the objectives, and background questions are asked to check and clarify his learning of that content. Then, content instruction finally leads to criterion performance of the objective. Finally, the student completes a post-test of all objectives of a given chapter or assignment. Added reference may be given with the post-test answers to other sources of content the student might want to read to clarify objectives not yet mastered, or the student is referred back into the text itself.

Outcomes Expected

The outcomes to be anticipated through the use of an Interactive Text could easily be summarized by saying that it increases learning effectiveness. The typical textbook, of a noninteractive nature, is much like a lecture—it is informational in purpose. It does not have the interaction necessary for students to ascertain whether they have learned. Obviously, a text in any form has one advantage over a lecture, in that the user can go back and re-read, while in a lecture he cannot rehear (unless he has a tape recorder). Quite often, this going back to re-read is a clear indication that the reader does not know if he or she has learned. Direct interaction via questions which measure the stated objectives is the means by which the reader can know immediately if he is learning. The principal outcome is learning effectiveness—students learn.

Learning efficiency can also be expected from the use of this design, and this efficiency increases when the design utilizes a pre-test. Efficiency might seem at first to be an inaccurate outcome to be expected, in that interaction would increase the amount of time necessary to complete the text, as opposed to a more conventional text without interaction. However, efficiency can also be judged against *the total learning effort required.* That is, since the effectiveness of instruction is increased so that students know they are learning, the amount of time necessary to re-read or seek other sources of instruction is reduced.

Efficiency is achieved in another, more subtle way. There is a tendency in reading to gloss over some content and to let attention wander. This often necessitates having to re-read. With active responding, this tendency to wander is reduced, because each student can readily determine if he has or has not learned. There is a conclusion drawn by the reader using an Interactive Text that "If I don't pay closer attention, I won't be able to respond correctly." Thus, greater attention to content presentation can be anticipated as an outcome in itself, and this also relates to the outcome of learning efficiency.

APPENDIX A

SOURCES ON
INSTRUCTIONAL TECHNOLOGY

Listed here are those sources that the author has personally found to be useful. Each communicates some of the more important concepts related to the design of instruction.

The list has been made intentionally small, so as to suggest *a basic set of library resource materials* for the instructional technology novice. They deal with both procedure and principles in the design of effective and efficient instruction. They are not, generally speaking, resources covering theory, but rather *practice*.

The sources are listed in alphabetical order, according to the authors. After each appear one or more of the symbols O, I, and V. "O" means that the source covers the topic and concepts related to behavioral objectives. "I" means that the source covers the wide range of topics related to interactive and individualized instruction. Finally, "V" means that the source covers the topic of validation.

Boston, Robert E. *How to Write and Use Performance Objectives to Individualize Instruction* (four booklets). Englewood Cliffs, New Jersey: Educational Technology Publications, 1972. O-I-V

Briggs, Leslie J. *Handbook of Procedures for the Design of Instruction.* Pittsburgh, Pennsylvania: American Institutes for Research, 1970. O-I-V

Butler, F. Coit. *Instructional Systems Development for Vocational and Technical Training.* Englewood Cliffs, New Jersey: Educational Technology Publications, 1972. O-I-V

Dillman, Caroline M. and Rahmlow, Harold F. *Writing Instructional Objectives.* Belmont, California: Fearon Publishers, 1972. O

Drumheller, Sidney J. *Handbook of Curriculum Design for Individualized Instruction—A Systems Approach: How to Develop Curriculum Materials from Rigorously Defined Behavioral Objectives.* Englewood Cliffs, New Jersey: Educational Technology Publications, 1971. O-I

Esbensen, Thorwald. *Working with Individualized Instruction.* Belmont, California: Fearon Publishers, 1968. O-I

Kapfer, Philip G. and Ovard, Glen F. *Preparing and Using Individualized Learning Packages for Ungraded, Continuous Progress Education.* Englewood Cliffs, New Jersey: Educational Technology Publications, 1971. O-I-V

Kemp, Jerrold E. *Instructional Design.* Belmont, California: Fearon Publishers, 1971. O-I-V

Mager, Robert F. *Preparing Instructional Objectives.* Belmont, California: Fearon Publishers, 1962. O

Designing Effective Instruction. An audio-filmstrip-workbook workshop. San Rafael, California: General Programmed Teaching, 1970. O-I-V

APPENDIX B

PROCEDURAL GUIDES

In the pages which follow, a basic outline is given of the procedure to follow in developing each instructional design discussed in this book.

It should be emphasized that each procedure is an outline of what is usually a much more elaborately drawn-out plan for program development. The intent is to show the recommended order in which components of a design should be developed. Each procedure begins with those developmental activities which center on defining what the student will learn (objectives) and how he will demonstrate learning mastery (criterion questions).

Generally, the procedures for program development are spelled out in much detail. Such detail is necessary so that all those concerned with the total program development effort will not overlook any of the critical activities to be completed. Such detail is also helpful in that developers can see where they are headed, plan their time most efficiently, and meet crucial due dates.

Detailed procedural guides contain more than just the parts of an instructional design to be developed and a listing of the order in which such parts are to be completed. The procedure should also specify the people responsible for completing a particular part of a design. Who will take responsibility? The procedure might also include people to be brought together for conferences or materials to be assembled (i.e., tests and profiles). These people, materials, conferences, and so forth are things usually unique to any given developmental effort. Thus, only an outline of recommended procedures is given. However, to give some idea of what other details are involved in a developmental procedure, *actual procedural guides* used to develop programs in the Audio-Workbook and Learner Controlled Instruction designs are included.

PROCEDURAL GUIDE

Learner Controlled Instruction

	UNIT							
	1	2	3	4	5	6	7	8
1. Project Team Assigned								
2. Conference								
3. Objectives Written								
4. Objectives Approved by								
5. Criterion Test Items Written								
6. Criterion Test Items Approved by								
7. Objectives Grouped by Major Units								
8. Objectives and Crt. Items Coded Together								
9. References Coded to Objectives								
10. Obj.—Reference Sheet Collated—Rough								
11. Student Guide Written								
12. Evaluator's Guide Written								
13. Test Copy Typing:								
Obj.—Ref. Sheets								
Criterion Tests								
Student Guide								
Eval. Guide								
14. Obj.—Ref. Sheets to Crit. Tests Proofed								
15. Test Copies Duplicated								
16. Test Copies Compiled								
17. Developmental Testing (date)								
18. Test Scored								
Test on Matrix								
Test Results Analyzed								
19. Conference on Test								
20. Revisions Completed								
21. Test Copies Duplicated								
22. Test Copies Compiled								
23. Field Testing (date)								
24. Test Scored								
Test on Matrix								
Test Results Analyzed								
25. Test Conference								
26. Revisions Completed								
27. Final Typing:								
Obj.—Ref. Sheets								
Criterion Tests								
Student Guide								
Evaluator's Guide								
28. Program Completed								

PROCEDURAL GUIDE

Interactive Lesson Plan or *Construct Lesson Plan*

	UNIT	1	2	3	4	5	6	7	8
Student Workbook	1. Objectives Written								
	2. Student Questions and Answers (to Objectives)								
	3. Background Questions and Answ.								
	4. Sequence Objectives within Major Topics								
	5. Add References to Objectives								
	6. Student Workbook Collated								
Lesson Plan	7. Objectives Subdivided for Lesson								
	8. Content Reminders Specified								
	9. Visual Aids Specified								
	10. Lesson Plan Collated								
	Content Breakdown								
	Instructions								
	Objectives								
	Content Reminders								
	Questions								
	Confirmations								
	11. Purpose and Significance Written								

PROCEDURAL GUIDE

Adjunct Study Guide

	UNIT 1	2	3	4	5	6	7	8
1. Objectives Written								
2. Terminal Questions and Answers Written								
3. Objectives and Questions Approved								
4. Sequence Objectives								
5. References Specified to Objectives								
6. Background Questions and Ans. Written								
7. Sequence and number 2, 5, 6 above—Sec. III Format								
8. Sequence Terminal Question Answers								
9. Summary Written—Section IV Format								
10. Obj.-Terminal Questions-Ans.—Summary Sequence Coding Check								
11. Objective List Finalized—Section II								
12. Cumulative Problem and Ans. Written—Sec. V								
13. Purpose and Significance Written—Sec. I								
14. Program Collated								
15. Program Completed								

PROCEDURAL GUIDE

Core Package

		UNIT 1	2	3	4	5	6	7	8
JOB SHEET	1. Terminal Objectives Written								
	2. Terminal Ques. and Answ. Written								
ASSIGN. SHEET	3. Enabling Objectives Written								
	4. Enabling Ques. and Answ. Written								
	5. Reference Specified								
	6. Gen. Infor. and Instructions Written								
	7. Procedure Written								
	8. Reference Written								
	9. Tools and Materials Specified								
	10. Gen. Infor. and Instructions Written								
MATH, SCIENCE, ETC., SHEETS	11. Relevance Objectives Written								
	12. Relev. Questions and Answ. Written								
	13. Procedure Written								
	14. Reference Specified								
	15. Tools and Materials Specified								
	16. Gen. Infor. and Instructions Written								
	17. Objective List Compiled								
	18. Purpose and Significance Written								
	19. Program Collated								

PROCEDURAL GUIDE

Tri-Level Study Guide

	UNIT	1	2	3	4	5	6	7	8
1.	Objectives Written								
2.	Criterion Test Items								
	As Specified by Objectives								
	Other example								
	Other form								
3.	Questions and Answ. Written								
4.	Instructions Written								
5.	Reference Specified								
6.	Gen. Information Written								

PROCEDURAL GUIDE

Audio-Workbook

	UNIT 1	2	3	4	5	6	7	8
1. Project Team Assigned								
2. Content Conference								
3. Questions and Ans. Written—SME								
Reviewed and Edit—Coor.								
4. Objectives Written—Prog.								
Objectives Approved—SME								
5. Obj. and Questions Reviewed—Coor.								
6. Record Content—SME								
Transcribe Recording—Sec.								
7. Script Edited—SME								
8. Questions, cues, etc., added—Prog.								
9. Criterion Test Written—Prog.								
Criterion Test Approved—SME								
10. 1st Draft Program Review—Coor.								
11. Script Typed—Sec.								
Script Proofed—Sec.								
12. Workbook Typed—Sec.								
Workbook Proofed—Sec.								
13. Script Recorded—Coor.								
Recording Proofed—Prog.								
Recording Approved—SME								
14. Workbook Xeroxed—Sec.								
Criterion Test Xeroxed—Sec.								
15. Test Draft Compiled—Coor.								
16. Developmental Testing (date)								
17. Test Scored—SME, Prog.								
Test Results on Matrix—Prog.								
Test Analyzed—Prog.								
18. Test Conference—Coor.								
19. Revisions Complete—Prog.								
Revisions Edit—SME								
20. Workbook Revisions Retyped—Sec.								
Script Revisions Retyped—Sec.								
21. Script Recorded—Coor.								
Recording Checked—Prog.								
Workbook Xeroxed—Sec.								
22. Tape & Workbook Check—Coor.								
23. Prepare								
_____# Tapes_____								
_____# Workbooks _____								
_____# Tests _____								
24. Field Test (date)								
25. Test Scored—SME, Prog.								
Test Results on Matrix—Prog.								
Test Analyzed—Prog.								
26. Test Conference—Coor.								
27. Revisions Complete—Prog.								
Revisions Edit—SME								
28. Final Okay—Coor.								

PROCEDURAL GUIDE

Interactive Text

	UNIT	1	2	3	4	5	6	7	8
1.	Objectives Written								
2.	Criterion Questions and Answ. Written								
3.	Background Questions and Answ. Written								
4.	Sequence Objectives								
5.	Content Written								
6.	Pre-Test Written								
7.	Post-Test Written								
8.	Program Complete								

ABOUT THE AUTHOR

Danny G. Langdon is Director of Instructional Design, Adult Learning Laboratory, American College of Life Underwriters, Bryn Mawr, Pennsylvania. Mr. Langdon carries on research and development activities related to improving the effectiveness and efficiency of learning.

Prior to his present position, Mr. Langdon was Administrative Assistant for Program Production, General Programmed Teaching Corporation, and Instructional Materials Supervisor, Parks Job Corps Center, Litton Industries.